Helen Ainslie Smith

History of Japan in Words of one Syllable

Helen Ainslie Smith

History of Japan in Words of one Syllable

ISBN/EAN: 9783337170967

Printed in Europe, USA, Canada, Australia, Japan

Cover: Foto ©ninafisch / pixelio.de

More available books at **www.hansebooks.com**

HISTORY OF JAPAN

IN WORDS OF ONE SYLLABLE

BY

HELEN AINSLIE SMITH

ILLUSTRATED

GEORGE ROUTLEDGE AND SONS
NEW YORK: 9 LAFAYETTE PLACE
LONDON: BROADWAY, LUDGATE HILL

IN UNIFORM STYLE,
Words of One Syllable.

ILLUSTRATED.

HISTORY OF ENGLAND.
HISTORY OF GERMANY.
HISTORY OF UNITED STATES.
HISTORY OF FRANCE.
LIVES OF THE PRESIDENTS OF THE UNITED STATES.
HISTORY OF IRELAND.
HISTORY OF RUSSIA.
HISTORY OF JAPAN.

GEORGE ROUTLEDGE & SONS,
9 Lafayette Place, New York.

Copyright, 1887,
BY JOSEPH L. BLAMIRE.

CONTENTS.

CHAPTER I.
THE FIRST RA-CES IN JA-PAN, . 7

CHAPTER II.
HOW THE MI-KA-DO'S EM-PIRE BE-CAME A REAL NA-TION, . 13

CHAPTER III.
LIFE AND WAYS IN AN-CIENT JA-PAN, . . . 22

CHAPTER IV.
TALES OF EAR-LY WARS, ... 37

CHAPTER V
JA-PAN'S FIRST FOR-EIGN CON-QUEST, ... 49

CHAPTER VI.
HOW JA-PAN FELL UN-DER MIL-I-TA-RY RULE, . . . 59

CHAPTER VII.
THE RULE OF THE HOUSE OF GEN, . . 74

CHAPTER VIII.
THE WAYS OF WAR IN FEU-DAL TIMES, ... 87

CHAPTER IX.
THE WAYS OF PEACE IN FEU-DAL TIMES, 100

CHAPTER X.
THE LONG SWAY OF THE HO-JO CLAN,

CHAPTER XI.
A BRIEF REIGN FOR THE MI-KA-DO,

CHAPTER XII.
NIT-TA AND KU-SUN-O-KI,

CHAPTER XIII.
THE ASH-I-KA-GA AGE,

CHAPTER XIV.
HI-DE-YOSH-I, OR THE AGE OF THE TAI-KO,

CHAPTER XV.
I-YE-YAS-U AND THE HOUSE OF TO-KU-JA-WA,

CHAPTER XVI.
THE LONG PEACE,

CHAPTER XVII.
THE LAST WAR AND THE DAWN OF A NEW AGE,

HISTORY OF JAPAN.

CHAPTER I.

THE FIRST RACES IN JAPAN.

The strong sea winds and the swift sea waves that still bear boats and men out of their course to the shores of the Ja-pan Isles, were the means, it is thought, by which men were first brought there from the old realms or tribes of the main land. It is said that the swift Black Stream, which flows from far out in the Pa-cif-ic up to the Sea of Ja-pan, as well as the great storms that vex the coast of A-si-a, have long brought boat-loads of folks from the south and west to the shores of Ki-u-shi-u, Shi-ko-ku, Hon-do, and the rest of the isles that now form the south end of the realm of Ja-pan. This land you know is made up of four large isles and a great host of small ones that lie off the east coast of A-si-a—with the Sea of Ja-pan be-tween, and forms a great bow-like chain that rounds out in the Pa-cif-ic. Chi-na and Co-re-a lie west of its south half, while off

Ye-zo and the North part of Nip-pon—the isle—the Rus-sian land swells out till the Sea is but a strait, and the hills and ports of the Tzar get a much more close view of the Mi-ka-do's realm than Chi-na has. It was to the south isles that the high seas and great winds drove the boat-men of the South; but, in the North lands there were bands of wild men who came down of their own will to Ye-zo and the isles near by. Some of these were from the East shores of A-si-a, and some of them may have gone from a long way in-land, where tales had spread to them of a land more fair to live in than their own, and of much good fish to be caught in the seas of these strange lands. It is known for a fact that these Ai-ni-noo men dwelt in Ye-zo, and it is the sons of their race who still live there. Those who first made their homes in Shi-ko-ku and Ki-u-shi-u were not from one race, as the men of Ye-zo, but came from ma-ny parts of the South of A-si-a and formed what we call a mixed race. Some time af-ter these men had found their way to Ja-pan, but far back in the past, when that great man of the Bi-ble, Neb-u-chad-nez-zar, was on the throne of Bab-y-lon, there came to the isles a great chief who first fought the tribes of wild men of Ki-u-shi-u and Shi-ko-ku, who dwelt in small towns, each in the rule of a head-man. When he had made them own him for their chief, he went on to Ye-zo and here had more hard fight to set his sway on the race from the North. But he won at last, though for a long time there was but one way by which they could be kept in check; this was by the force of the new chief's vast troops. The strife, which first rose more than two thou-sand years a-go, was kept up for

DO-MES-TIC SCENE.

scores and scores of years; but the race of the new chief put down their foes in the end, and then all the ra-ces on the isles grew to be one, and that was the Jap-a-nese.

This realm, which grew in time to be large and great, was first set up by Jim-mu Ten-no, 660 years ere Christ was born, and as it still stands, it is now near 2250 years old, and Mut-su-hi-to, the Mi-ka-do or great chief, who now sits on its throne, is the 123d em-pe-ror of his race.

Though there are tales of what took place ere Jim-mu came and set up his realm in the midst of the first men, naught at all is known for fact ere the year 660 B. C., and much that is said of Jim-mu and some of the sons of his race who came in his line for a long time, is naught but tales; and though these form a part of the sto-ry of the growth of the realm, all folks on our side of the globe at least, know that they must not be read for truth.

The Jap-a-nese think that heav-en and earth were once all one, and that the sun and the moon were god-dess-es that were born to a life that has no end, at the time when the earth and heav-en first grew to be in two parts; and they think, too, that there were more gods and god-dess-es born at this time, and that Jim-mu was one of them, and that he came (in the year 660) from the great and ho-ly mount of Kir-i-shi-ma, which is on the way from Hi-u-ga to O-zu-mi. All the Jap-a-nese small folks are taught to look with awe on that fair height which lifts its head far a-bove the clouds, and to think of the time when the god Jim-mu came down to it out of the blue sky of heav-en, that seems so near its peak, and set up on

earth the realm of the Mi-ka-do, and gave Ja-pan a
line of em-pe-rors that still sit on its throne. That
is why all the Jap-a-nese think their em-pe-ror,
and all his race are born gods and can do no

BALL GAME.

wrong, and that their souls go back to dwell in the
sky when they die.

The tale is that when Jim-mu had made him-self
lord of the whole land, his next step was to set up

his chief town, and for that he chose the site of Kash-i-wa-ba-ra, which is some miles from where the town of Ki-o-to now stands. Here he set up a sort of court, gave states or parts of the realm to the charge of his chief men-at-arms, made gifts to his troops in pay for their good work with the foe; and set out at once to give peace and good rule to his new realm. It was his wish to bring all the folks of the land to feel that they were all a part of one great state, to put off war-like ways, and to learn the arts of peace. He took a wife, the Princess Ta-ta-ra, and set the type of a good home-life. His rule was long and wise. When he was near a hun-dred and thir-ty years old he died and left three sons. We can not be at all sure that this man dwelt on earth, but the Jap-a-nese have been taught to think that he was a real man; they think he is now a god, whom it is part of their faith to love and bow down to; the em-pe-ror now on the throne speaks of him as his sire, and claims that he is come from Jim-mu, and is his son through a long line in which there has been no break. The first year of Jap-a-nese his-to-ry is set down as that on which he took the throne at Kash-i-wa-ba-ra, and the day is kept (like our own 4th of Ju-ly) each year on the 7th day of the 4th month, or as we would say, on the 7th of A-pril.

CHAPTER II.

HOW THE MIKADO'S EMPIRE BECAME A REAL NATION.

From the first the Mi-ka-dos have had the right to name whom they choose to take the throne when they should die or have to leave it; and though as a rule it goes to the first son, the son has to wait for his sire to name him or to bide by his will if he thinks best to name one of his broth-ers. Jim-mu left his throne to one of his three sons when he died. He, in turn, left it to one of his sons, and so it was with a long line of whom we do not know much that is truth, though their names and some dates have been kept with great care in the list of the Mi-ka-dos; and one of the first who wrote Jap-a-nese his-to-ry tells long tales of their reigns and great deeds. Most of them were more than a hun-dred years old when they died, and one of them is said to have been on the throne for a hun-dred and one years. Of all the eight kings who sat on the throne in the years that passed from the time of Jim-mu till the date when Christ was born in the lands of the

West (which was not thought of nor heard of in Ja-pan), the chief Mi-ka-do of note was Su-jin, whose reign was for more than half the cent-u-ry that came to an end with the birth of Christ. He was both brave and good, and gave much thought to the gods, we are told; and by him the rough tribes of the isles were made much more like a real na-tion than they had been ere this. Up to this time the Jap-a-nese were but a half-wild host, made up of folks from most all the lands near them. They were rude and strong, fond of sports, and in all ways much like the tribes of the East of those old times; but they left off their wild and rough ways more soon than most of them. To win in war made a man great and gave him strength and force with those who knew him. This Su-jin had done in the days of his youth, and so he was the more able to lift his folks up when he came to be Mi-ka-do, for they felt that they could trust him to lead them. It was due to his zeal that the old faith of the realm which had come with Jim-mu was kept up; for folks had grown not to think of their gods by this time; but this prince made much of the rites and all that was due to the faith of his sires; and he built it up so strong that from that time to this it has kept a great hold on the Jap-a-nese.

The folks had grown in-to some wrong ways since

A NO-BLE TRAV-EL-ING.

the days of Jim-mu; they did not think of their gods and some of them did not try to do right nor to please those who dwelt in the sky, and had sent down Jim-mu and his race to live in and rule Ja-pan. This gave the good Su-jin much grief. He sent calls to the folks to give up their bad ways and be good, but they did not heed him, till a great plague came, which, the Jap-a-nese say, the gods would not check till the king made long fasts and prayed much to them, and had a great rite in view of "all the world"—that is Ja-pan, for in old times the Jap-a-nese thought their realm was the whole earth. When the plague did stop (which must have been when it could spread no more, or at a change in the weath-er), the folks were much struck with the signs of how great were their gods and their own sins; and they then took heed of the Mi-ka-do's call, and sought to do the will of the gods with great zeal. By this means Su-jin soon did a great deal to raise the realm from the rough state in which he had found it to peace, good rule, and all the fine things for a realm which are meant by the one big word civ-il-i-za-tion. There were in the house of the Mi-ka-do a mir-ror, a sword, and a ball, which Jim-mu had put there with much care as the "sa-cred em-blems" of his god-race,—that is, things which the Mi-ka-do and all the men of the land were to look on as the

type of what was most high to them — some-what as
Ro-man Cath-o-lics look on the cross. These Su-jin
sent out of his house for fear it was not well for them
to be so near him (for his bod-y was but of earth
though his soul was of heav-en;) and, while he had
a mir-ror, a sword, and a ball made just like them
and put in a " place of rev-er-ence" made for them
in his own house, the real em-blems were put in a
small church built for them far off from the house of
an-y man, where they could not be hurt in the least
by aught that was not pure; then he made his own
girl-child a priest-ess to take care of them — and to
this day these things are in the shrines of U-ji
in I-se — where they were put in the year 4 A. D.
They are still kept in the charge of a maid who
is of the race of the Mi-ka-do and can not wed.
The small church, or tem-ple, which the Mi-ka-do
built for the cop-ies of the em-blems was the first of
the shrines that have since been put up as a part of
each roy-al house that has been raised in Ja-pan.

Su-jin's zeal for the good of the realm came out in
more than one way. He did as much for its trade,
its growth in wealth and strength as a state, as for
the true faith. He made a law that all the men and
the wom-en of the realm should — each for a short
time — leave their own work and give a share of
their toil to the realm, the work of the men went for

the troops while that of the wom-en was at their looms or in the field. This wise king did a great deal to put good new ways of life in the place of the old ones the men had learned from their sires of the half-wild tribes of A-si-a. To make a just plan for them to pay their tax he had the first lists made out of the folks in all parts of the land, which was the same scheme as that by which a cen-sus, as we call it, is made in our own land each ten years or so; and he taught them, too, how to keep a count of time. For Su-jin to think this out for him-self shows that he was a man of a great mind. He had boats built, too; and did all he could to try to make the folks work more and do more, to take more in their boat-loads when they set out with fish or the stuff that they made or raised in their fields to oth-er ports to change for things they could not raise. In this way they built up trade and their wealth grew year by year as time went on; then he taught them to make more of their land than they had known how to ere this, so that he is now known as the fath-er of Jap-a-nese farm-ing. He made ca-nals him-self and sent forth word that his folks should dig them, too, so that the fields of rice need not want for wa-ter. This made the rice crops more large than they had been, but there were more boats to bear it to parts of the realm where it did not grow, and in this way the men of the north and south, east and west, came to deal with and to know each oth-er. This kept them so that they did not grow not to care for an-y part of the realm but just that where they dwelt, which does a realm great harm. You

SHOPS AND WARE-HOUS-ES.

can see by this that the rice trade of Ja-pan is an old one as well as a large one. There are vast fields of flat lands with huge tanks full of wa-ter to be let out on the field when the right time comes — for rice is grown as well as sown in wa-ter; and the hill-sides, too, are some-times cut so as to form sta-ges like great flights of steps, and more than one swift stream is turned from its wild course to flow smooth and calm through a long ditch cut through the rice-fields of the hill-sides.

There was naught, it seems, that this good Mi-ka-do did not think of for his realm. Home work, home trade, good laws, were not all that he left his folks. He made friends with Co-re-a, and let one of the great chiefs of that realm of the West come a-cross the Sea of Ja-pan and live on his lands; and he learnt from his guest good things which he made use of in his realm. As there were yet in the North part of the isles some wild tribes of the Ai-no's or first men of the land, who still held out as foes of the Jap-a-nese, and with whom these good farm folks of Yu-ma-to were in a sort of line-war all the time, Su-jin made up his mind to put the whole realm in charge of troops to guard its bounds and to keep its men and their homes safe from the foe. The whole land was marked off in-to four parts, and each part was put in the charge of a chief man-at-arms, which the Jap-a-nese call a Sho-gun, and which we would call a gen-e-ral. This was the first stage of the Mi-ka-do's troop which grew great as years went on, and which came at last to claim a large class from the Jap-a-nese race. But at first the ranks were made up from the hands in the field, the trades-men, and from all the folks, who left their work and went out to fight un-der the Mi-ka-do them-selves, when there was a call to war, and who took their way back home as soon as it was done.

It was in the reign of the next king that store-hous-es were set up in the realm, and that some such plans as those for the troops of our own day were made to keep food and arms on hand so that the men could set out at an-y time to put down an out-break of their foes, or quell an-y such ill in their own lands—for some of the Mi-ka-do's own men were not yet much less rough and wild than those of the tribes from which they had sprung. In the far-off parts of the realm there had to be a strict watch kept on them all the time, or they would rise in host and break out in much the same sort of fights as we still have to dread from our red men of the West. Some one who has dwelt in Ja-pan and knows its tale well, says that the Mi-ka-do's realm grew by war and fire and blood-shed, very much as our own race first got its hold on the land of the red men. The Jap-a-nese were war-like men from the first, and it was in the camps and field near the lines of their wild foes that their race of men-at-arms grew and learnt to love war and to live for naught but that, and to know all its arts and have so much more skill in them than the sons of oth-er parts of the

East. It was this ar-my plan, too, which did a great deal to bind all parts of the realm in-to one em-pire, so that it grew in strength as it grew in size, which it could not have done if it had been cut up in parts that spent their life in home-wars.

CHAPTER III.

LIFE AND WAYS IN ANCIENT JAPAN.

The life and laws and ways of the Jap-a-nese have seen less change since the time of the first Mi-ka-dos than those of most lands, though in all the East there has been far less change, from age to age, than has come in the same length of time to Eu-rope and all lands of the West. In the first place, the Jap-a-nese got a good start; they were far less rude as a race than most of the tribes in that part of A-si-a, and so have had less to learn than they. Two, at least, of their first Mi-ka-dos were great men, who thought out wise plans by which they built up a strong realm, whose many parts were bound in-to one great whole by firm ties. One man ruled them all; he was the head of their state as well as their faith, and was a son of the ho-ly race which had been sent from on high to rule them and take care of their realm. But, with all this, if the Jap-a-nese had made friends with and learned the thoughts and plans of the men of oth-er lands, they could not have kept so firm in their own way, and it is due to that more than aught else that their realm was not split up and torn by bad home wars and that in the long lapse of years, when great

SLEEP-ING ON BLOCK PIL-LOWS.

ills fell on the lands west of Ja-pan and vast chang-es of all sorts shook near all the rest of the earth, this realm of sea-isles kept on in her own way and grew more large and more strong age by age, with not more than three or four such great chang-es as Rus-sia, France and Prus-sia had all the time in the course of near a score of cent-u-ries.

Jim-mu had found these isles a realm most fair to see. In the East and North its moors lay in long tracts of grass and reeds and bam-boo cane, where wild beasts dwelt and gave the sports of the chase to the wild men of the soil. Its steep hills and its calm dells were grand and fair, and some-times set thick with trees and green with grass or grown with wild flow-ers. Its men dwelt in small huts that stood in groups; they had no tame beasts; their ways of life were rude and wild; they could fish and hunt, but they did not know how to do much else. In the course of time they learned to till their ground, for the race of Jim-mu knew how to raise crops and work ores, which were found to lie in the earth of these isles. The men soon learned to dig for them and then to work them; and their wives learned how to weave and to spin; and then some of the men bought and sold the fruits of the soil and the goods that were made; and so trade grew, and with that all learned to put forth their strength to raise more and more each year, or to push on and make some thing more fine than had been yet tried; and so arts grew and sci-ence, and ere long the folks who dwelt near the Mi-ka-do's court or in or near the large towns had quite left off their old rude ways and were like a new race.

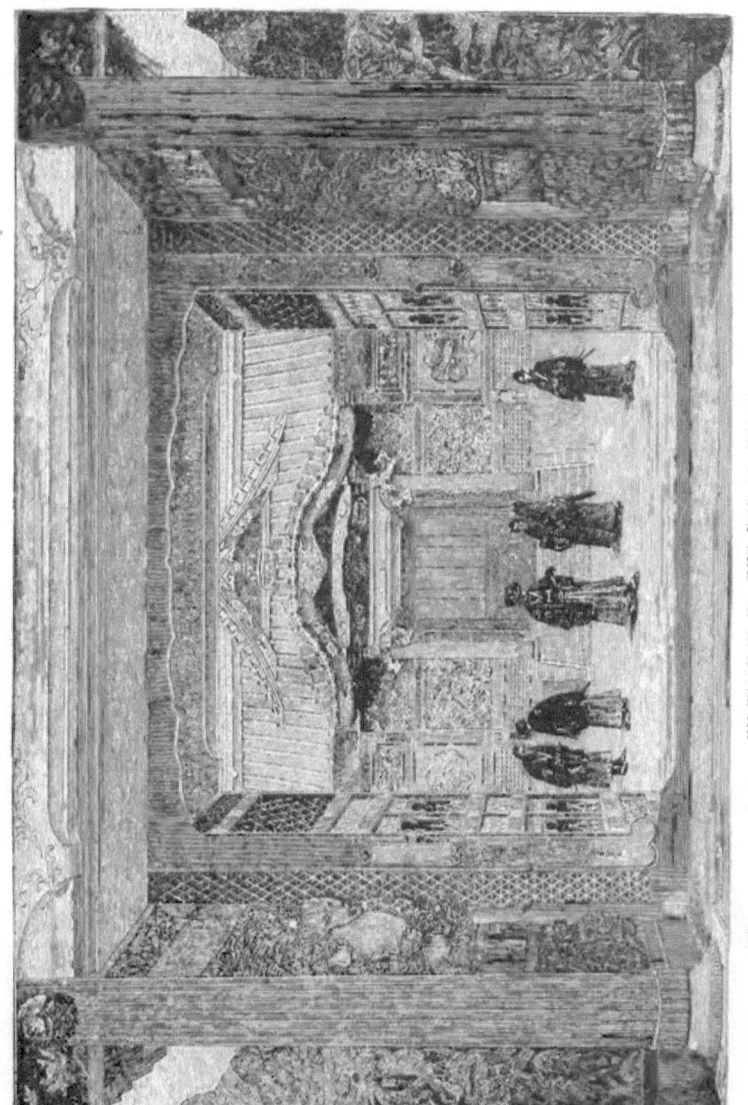

ENTRANCE TO THE ROYAL TOMB.

Like all wild men, the first Jap-a-nese thought that an-y one who was so brave and so great that he could lead in wars and win in large fights must be a god ; and so when Jim-mu beat the tribes of the South and some of the strong Ai-nos, and then set up his realm in the midst of them and made him-self chief lord of the sea-girt isles, it was not hard for him to make the tribes whom he had o-ver-come think he had been sent from on high and that he had full rights to rule them. If he was a god, so were his sons and all the chil-dren of his line. From this grew the first Jap-a-nese faith, which is known as the Shin-to. It is yet one of the chief faiths of the land, and those who hold to it still think that the Mi-ka-do is the son of the great sun-god-dess, who is at the head of all that they pray to. But there is more than one god in Shin-to. Those who hold to it think that all their great men who have fought in all the wars of the realm are gods. They bow down and pray to their sires as well as their kings, to their wise men and all who have done great work of an-y kind for Ja-pan, while more high than all these they hold the sun or light —which they look on as a god-dess—and fire and most of the forc-es of na-ture,—that is, rain and wind and all those things with-out which all that now has life on the earth would die. Each fief, each town, all parts of the land, have their own saints or *ka-mi*, and the whole realm is now set thick with shrines, and there seems no end to the gods and half-gods of the Shin-to. But at first the folks did not have all these way-side shrines that now dot the whole land. The first men met on the hill-top, on the banks of the streams and in the woods to lay fruits, fish, and game on a rude shrine of stone or earth, and give them to their gods in thanks for what they had had or when they would pray for what they were in want of. They still have no i-dols, but they had priests in those days as now, who wore white robes, made themselves clean in the bath, and took no food ere they laid these gifts of men on the shrines of the gods.

The first law of this old faith is that those who hold to it must be clean and pure. The priests have to bathe a great deal and to put on clean clothes ere they go to pray or to their ho-ly work, and all who walk in it are bound to keep themselves from all that is not thought to be pure and clean.

At first none but the Mi-ka-do had a shrine to the sun-god-dess, but ere long a few were set up to her in the towns or where a few farm-folks dwelt in a group of huts, and at last there came to be a great ma-ny to her. Then there were tem-ples; but it was a long time ere the way-side shrines that one now sees in all parts of the land were set up in the woods or on the roads through the hills or tracts of farm lands.

Twice a year, in the Sixth and Twelfth months, the folks of the old times met on the banks of a stream and there had a great Shin-to rite. It was the time when all the realm could be made clean of its sins and its wrong ways, when men could bathe in the stream and pray and be pure. The odes that were made up to be sung to the gods at these rites were the first that are known to have been made in the Jap-a-nese tongue. The form of pray-er that they then had is still in use by those who hold the Shin-to faith. But this and the odes were not kept in writ-ing. The Jap-a-nese of that day did not know how to write in an-y way, not e-ven by signs. Men taught their sons what they knew, and so for a long, long time all the his-to-ry, laws, tales and odes or an-y sort of verse of the Jap-a-nese were kept in the minds of a few, who passed them from sire to son, till some one thought of a way to write them down. Most of the world has learnt to draw and paint and to make statues and has got most all of this kind of art from Greece, but the art of the Jap-a-nese is all their own. It was born in them, and is not like that of an-y oth-er folks in the world.

From the first they have known how to do their work in met-als, and in chi-na, which is more fine than the men of any oth-er land have made or can make; but the world of the West had known the fine arts for a long time ere the Jap-a-nese seem to have thought that they could make cop-ies of men

AN ART-IST AT WORK.

and beasts in clay or wood or that they could draw or paint scenes of their folks, their life and their land. When they did wake to this, it was in the reign of Su-jin or his son, and was near the time that Christ came to live on earth. There was a cus-tom in the land that when a lord or great man died, his wife and one or two serv-ants should die and be put in the grave with him. The son of Su-jin tried to put a stop to this hard rite and did check it, but not quite. In a few years af-ter he sent out word to have it done no more, the Em-press died, and the folks of the land would have felt that it was not at all right to put her in the grave a-lone, but one of the men of the court who had made some fig-ures of clay was a-ble to have these put in the place of the real bod-ies. The Mi-ka-do was glad to hail this new plan; he would raise the man who made the fig-ures to a high place and gave him the name of Ha-ji, which means one who knows the art by which clay im-a-ges are made. That put an end to the law that one man should die to be put in the grave with some one else, and it was the birth of fine art in Ja-pan. But it was a long time ere the folks of that land did an-y more than rude work of this kind. There is no place in the world where men can do such fine work as the Jap-a-nese have long done in their use of met-als, in chi-na and lac-quer-ware and in the way they weave silks and make it up in clothes; but for a long time they did not do much in the fine arts that are best known to the West. In time they learnt how to carve fig-ures as well as to form them out of clay; and they draw men and beasts with a more free and true hand than the art-ists of Eu-rope have; but they have had to learn how to draw out-door scenes—so as to make them look right—in the last few years, and they did not know at all how to paint in oils. But they use their own col-ors with as much if not more skill than the best paint-ers of old times or late years.

In the days of long a-go the first Jap-a-nese dwelt in small huts which they made for them-selves. To build them, they stuck the poles of young trees with the bark still on them straight up in the ground and a-cross them bound more poles with a sort of rope made of vines or a rush that grew wild in pools near by. This made the frame, on which they put walls made of mats of grass, of boughs or of rush, while on the bam-boo frame-work of the peak roof they put a thick thatch which was of grass. The floors were of hard earth while doors and win-dows were holes, o-ver which mats were some-times hung. They were most plain in all ways, and in that they were like the Mi-ka-do's own home, for though this had more size than the huts of the folks, it was in old times as now a plain house with naught in it for show. For a long time it was no more fine or grand than those of his lords, and but for its size and that it stood a bit more high, you could not have told it from a tem-ple or from the homes of most an-y of the high class folks of the Jap-a-nese realm. Since it was the place where dwelt a man who was thought to be half a god, it was much like a tem-ple, and as is still the rule with the Shin-to, all that has an-y part with that faith has no need to make a show of wealth or pomp. So in his life, his home, his dress and all else the Mi-ka-do was most plain. The shrines of the Shin-to faith of to-day are built on the same plan as the huts of these first men of the realm, and the homes one now sees there are on the same plan, too, though they are built with more size and more taste and have some good chang-es. The dress of those old times was made of the skins of wild beasts, and a coarse stuff that they wove of straw, grass, bark, and the fi-ber of the palm-tree. For a long time the folks knew naught of the silks and the cot-ton goods that are now worn so much in Ja-pan. Their dress was scant and plain; some of the time they wore a long cloak, with a belt, with leg-gings and san-dals of straw. As that was a-bout all they had for a full suit, there were, of course, times when less than that was worn. Their chief work was to hunt and fish; and their food was the flesh of deer or bears and most all the beasts that were wild in the woods, while they al-so had much fish and the roots of plants. It was a long time ere the faith of Bud-dha was brought in-to the land to teach them it was not right for them to eat the flesh of beasts; but when that time did come, they were taught to plant grain and use that for food. From the first, fish has been the chief food of the Jap-a-nese and that is why most of the folks have made their homes and their towns on the line of streams and near the sea.

The good work that Su-jin be-gan when he led

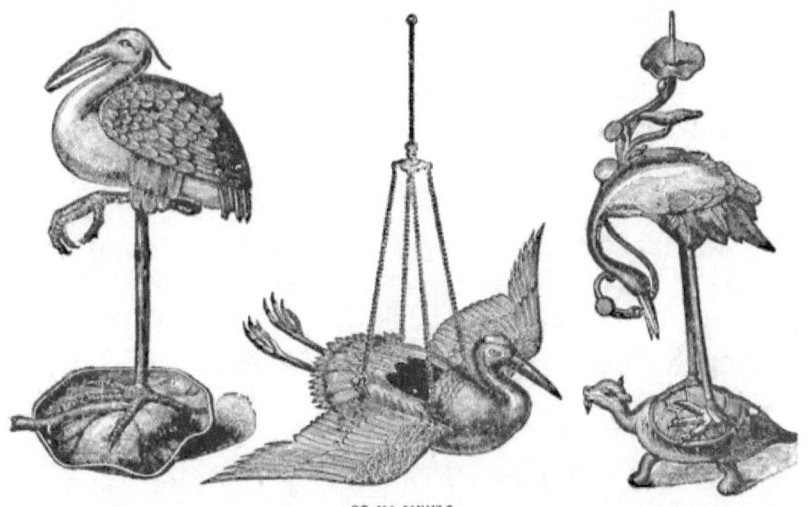

OR-NA-MENTS.

his men to work their fields and raise all the fine crops they could, has been kept up in all the times since, and now, in the tracts where folks live, through all the length and breadth of those fair isles, there is scarce an inch of ground that is good, or could be made so, that has not been put to the ver-y best use for crops. If you should go to Ja-pan, to the farm lands, you would see miles of hills and vales whose sides are made into stag-es, like tall pairs of broad stairs, for rice fields, you would see tracts of good, rich ground, with a vast net-work of tanks and wa-ter way spread through them, and broad tracts of green flat lands with not a fence on them, nor an-y beast, wild or tame, to harm them. In all this you would see what two thou-sand years of hard toil and great care has done to make the land do its ver-y best to bear rich fruits and great crops.

Jim-mu and his sons did not mean to let an-y part of the realm he had won from the first men of the isles slip from their hands; so a plan was soon made to hold it all in the sway of the "great lord." This plan was to mark off the land in sort of states or fiefs, each of which was put in the charge of a prince or chief, who was to take care that his folks did not break from the Mi-ka-do, and at the same time look out for their good in all the ways that the Mi-ka-do should think best. Some-times these head-men were lords of the Mi-ka-do's own tribe, and some-times they were chiefs of the tribes that Jim-mu had found in the land; all of them were like small kings in their own fiefs; they had their lands and their men; and no one but the Mi-ka-do was o-ver them. To him they had to pay a tax, and to him they had to

GIV-ING MON-EY TO THE PEO-PLE.

bow as their great lord. Some of the Ai-no chiefs did not quite like to own the sway of the Mi-ka-do, and the his-to-ry of the first years of the Jap-a-nese em-pire is full of tales of how now one, now more, broke out in vain tri-als to throw off the yoke. The space of land be-tween Lake Bi-wa and the bays of O-za-ka and O-wa-ri was known as the Ki-na-i, or Five Home States, and were the Mi-ka-do's own fiefs in his sole rule. The folks of these lands were bound to him by firm, strong ties; but in Shi-ko-ku and Ki-ush-i-u, of the South Isles, and the tribes that dwelt in the far West, North and East, were not yet quite put down. These fiefs were held by their own chiefs, who were on good terms with the Mi-ka-do, and paid court to him as their "Su-ze-rain," or head chief. When they got in feuds with each oth-er they would a-gree to take the case to him, and bide by what he said; for he was so strong at arms, and his realm took up so much of the best part of the isles that they would have had to look on him as their grand chief an-y way, but more than that, they all felt that he had come from heav-en; and so there was no one a-bove him to whom they could go. So he held his rank, and when word came from him the tribes would hear and heed his voice, though they might be in the midst of one of their worst feuds.

CHAPTER IV.

TALES OF EARLY WARS.

When Su-jin came to name the next em-per-or, the one who should take his place at his death, he found it hard to say which of his two sons he would choose. His love for both of them was the same, and he could not make up his mind to be more good to one than to the oth-er. At last he thought of a plan by which he could find out which of them would make the best em-per-or ; and one day he told them that they should come to him the next day and tell him what they dreamt that night. So when they had been through their bath and put on all clean night clothes, they laid down to sleep and to dream the dreams that would fix their fate. The next day they went to their great and good sire, and the first son said, he dreamt that he went up a high mount, and when he got to the top he stood, so he saw far off to the East, and that he cut with his sword and thrust with his spear eight times. Then the sire would hear what Su-i-nin, his young-er son, had dreamt. He too had gone up the high mount, but he had stretched cords and snares on all sides of him, and tried to catch the birds that ate the grain. Then the em-per-or thought what these dreams could mean, and at last he said to his first son, that since he had looked but one way he would go to the East and be the chief of that part of the realm; but Su-i-nin looked round him on all sides, and he should be chief of all. "You, my son, will be my heir," he said. So it was: the first son came to be the chief of the East and a great man at arms, while his broth-er took the throne, kept up the good work of his sire, and lived to reign in peace for near a hun-dred years. Ere he died, Christ was born in the West, and it was in the year 70, A. D., that he left his rule in the hands of Ke-i-ko, whose reign was made great by the deeds of his son.

This brave youth, Ya-ma-to-Da-ke, the son of the twelfth em-per-or of Ja-pan, was fine to look at, as well as bold to fight, and his quick wit took him where his strong sword could not. The tales that are told of him, which most of the Jap-a-nese of this day hold to be true, are quaint and old, and show us more of the strange forms of the Jap-a-nese faith than of real facts in their his-to-ry; but we are most sure that such a prince as Ya-ma-to-Da-ke did once dwell in the sea-girt realm, and that he did fight great wars in the isles of the South and East, and bring large tribes of the Ai-nos to own his father's sway.

It is said that he was brave and fond of war while he was yet a boy, and that in his youth he led a large force to put down an out-break of the rude folks that dwelt in the isle of Ki-ush-i-u. When he got there he found that the foes were in camp, and his next wish was to find their chief. So he made him-self look like a girl, who would dance for the chief, for he was fair and full of grace; and in that guise he went to the guard of the camp, who thought so fair and sweet a girl would please the chief, and took the young prince to his

EM-PER-OR IN AN-CIENT TIMES.

lord at once. The chief did like the girl, and drew her to his own tent, where he soon found that his guest had come for a feat that was much more stern than a dance, for the brave youth threw off his guise and laid hold of the chief, and took his life. This put an end to the strife in Ki-ush-i-u, and gave the prince the name of Ya-ma-to-Da-ke, which means war-like. It was more than ten years ere he set out on his next great war. That was in the year 110, A. D., when the tribes in the East part of Ja-pan broke out in wrath for the Mi-ka-do and his men-at-arms. The prince at the head of his troops went to put them down.

He gave word for his men to halt when they got to I-se, and there he went to the shrine of the Sun-god-dess where the sym-bols were kept (and are still), and while he left his own sword at the foot of the pine tree (all the shrines have a pine tree near them), he bore off that of the shrine which the good priest-ess gave him to fight his ho-ly war. With this to aid him in his cause, he led the way on to the wilds of Su-ra-ga to fight the rough Ai-nos. But, when they found he was near, they fled from the plains to the woods and the safe spots in the hills, for the Ai-nos fought much as our red-men do. They would not come to a fray in the field where both sides could meet on the same ground, but they would hide and, with trees or thick brush, or some great rocks in front of them, they would shoot darts at their foes while they kept them-selves out of sight. There was no trick they were so fond of as to make their foes get lost in the thick woods, where they were so much at home. They would hide them-selves in the coat of some wild beast, and thus act as spies and scouts while they made their guise cheat their foes and serve to trap them. Then, too, they would creep by stealth to the camp of the foe and set fire to the tents. At last, when they had drawn Ya-ma-to-Da-ke up in their woods and high haunts in the hills, they set fire to the growth of brush that stood thick on the ground, and it was joy to them to see how the wind drove the flames on and on to the camp of the Jap-a-nese troops. But, the tale says, when they had come so near that the prince thought his force would all be lost, the Sun-god-dess came to him, and he cut the grass round him with his ho-ly sword; and so great was its might that the flames swept on no more, but as if they had had a check, they stood still, and then ran back to where the bands of Ai-nos were hid, and burnt all those that did not at once run off and leave the land to the prince. Ya-ma-to-Da-ke gave thanks to the gods for this, and from that time the ho-ly sword no more bore the old name of "Cloud-clus-ter," which it had had since the days of Jim-mu; the prince gave it a new name, the "Grass-mow-er."

When he had made his gifts to the gods, he set out to push his way far through the lands of the Ai-nos and to add the great plain of the East, now known as the Ku-an-to, to the Mi-ka-do's realm. First he had to cross the Ha-ko-ne Mount-ains, and then he went on through the plain till he got to the Bay of Yed-do. He thought, as this was a strait of no great width, that he could take his troops with ease to the land be-yond, whose hills he could see so plain from the shore where he stood. But the brave prince did not know what winds and tides surge through the straits in that part of the bay, and with all his hosts he soon set out on a trip that was one of great fear and grief ere it came to an end. A storm came up, the seas rose high, and the poor boats were used so ill that the folks thought they would be lost. The prince was in a great fright; he thought that the sea-god did not like some-thing he had said, and that he had sent this storm to smite him. If that were so, there was but one way to check the storm: that was to make some gift to the god, and so put an end to his wrath. It had to be some great gift too, some man or wom-an, and it was hard to choose whom it should be. But the prince did not have to make the choice. His fair wife, Ta-chi-ba-na Hi-me, said she would give her-self to the sea-god for the sake of the rest, and when she had said good-by to the prince, she left him in deep grief, and with one leap from their boat she was lost in the mad waves. The sea drove the boat on for a time, but soon the storm died down, the sky grew clear, the bay calm, and the boat made for the shore. The new land to which Ya-ma-to-Da-ke had come was Kad-zu-sa, and he soon made him-self lord of the tribes he found there. In the bounds of the great town of To-ki-o, now at the head of this land, the site is still shown where the bold prince found his wife's comb, which was made of some wood of sweet scent, and which had lain on the top of the waves till they bore it to the shore. He built a shrine on the spot where he found it, and left the comb in it as a gift to the gods; and on that spot a Shin-to shrine still stands, where the men who fish and live on the bay go to pray to the souls of the

エ wo(e)	サ sa	ケ ke	井 wi(i)	ツ tsu	ワ wa	ト to	イ i
ヒ hi	キ ki	フ fu	ノ no	子 ne	カ ka	チ chi	ロ ro
モ mo	ユ yu	コ ko	オ o	ナ na	ヨ yo	リ ri	ハ ha
セ se	メ me	エ ye(e)	ク ku	ラ ra	タ ta	ヌ nu	ニ ni
ス su	ミ mi	テ te	ヤ ya	ム mu	レ re	ル ru	ホ ho
ン n	シ shi	ア a	マ ma	ウ u	ソ so	ヲ wo	ヘ he

SIGN AL-PHA-BET.

prince and his fair wife who gave her life for the boat-load that brought this land to own the Mi-ka-do's rule.

When this shrine was built and when he had the tribes well in hand, he set out to add more lands and more folks to the em-pire. He went to the north, through Shi-mo-sa, and with his hosts with him, kept on up the coast till he got to what the Jap-a-nese held to be the bounds of their realm. If you find the 38th par-al-lel on your maps, you will know as near as an-y one does where this was. In the lands on the north side of this line dwelt wild Ai-no tribes who were proud of their race, of their right to their lands, and of their might and free state. When they heard that a great prince was come from Ja-pan to put them down, they brought a vast host to meet him and show him that he must fight hard ere he did with them as with the men of Kad-zu-sa. Their first chiefs at the head of the hosts were on the shore in wait for the prince when his fleet came in view. It was a sight they had not seen nor dreamt of—this crowd of boats, with their full sails that bore for the shore by some strange force that they could not see. "From the gods!" they cried, "we shall die if we draw bow on them." And so when Ya-ma-to-Da-ke set foot on the strand, the proud fierce chiefs fell down in awe, and with ease he brought all the tribes to own his lord, the Mi-ka-do, as their great chief.

He was now glad to go back to his sire and his friends, but he did not take the most quick way to get to them, for it was his wish to learn as much as he could of this new land of the East. The tale which the Jap-a-nese tell of this long home-ward

IN-TE-RI-OR OF THE TEM-PLE.

trip is full of strange things. They tell how he went through some of the lands he had won on his way up; how, while he took rest at Ka-i, he made the first dis-tich or po-em, of thir-ty-one syl-la-bles, which is much used now-a-days. They tell how he sent one of his chiefs from here to make peace in the North-west, while he went on to Shi-na-no, a great stretch of high land, round which range some of the most high peaks and chains of mount-ains in all Ja-pan. He took his men through the pass of Us-u-i To-ge, which has a wide fame with all who have been to these isles, and while he stood on some high point from which he could see the view of plain and hills and sea that spread out at his feet — as fair a one as there is in Ja-pan—he thought of his lost wife, and in soft, low tones he said, "Ad-zu-ma! Ad-zu-ma!" which means, "My wife! My wife!" and to this day Ad-zu-ma is the name that po-ets give to the plains of Yed-do.

It was a task such as had not been tried ere this, to cross the great hills of Shi-na-no. There were no paths, and no one but the bold prince would have thought he could pick out a way through those steep, bright, smooth, la-va beds, swift streams and dense fogs. The folks thought that the place was full of gods, and each loose stone by which they lost their hold on a ledge of rock, each fog or thick cloud that fell on them, and all the bad smells from the gas of the earth or the peaks that sent forth fire were signs of the wrath of some god. Once when a white deer came up to Ya-ma-to-Da-ke, it was said that this was the bad god of the hills come to vex him. He threw some wild gar-lic in its eyes, from which it died. Then fog and mist spread in the path of his host, so they would have met their death there if it had not been that a good god, in the form of a white dog, led them to the plains of Mi-no. Then when they got near some foul gas, it was thought that the soul of the white deer had come on them,

A TEM-PLE.

so that they were too weak to stand, which naught but the wild gar-lic that the men ate could drive off. When they had gone through the plains of Mi-no and come to the tall mount of I-bu-ki Ka-ma, which rears its great flat head far through the clouds, Ya-ma-to-Da-ke made up his mind to break the strength of the bad gods who dwelt on this mount, and while he left his ho-ly sword, Grass-mow-er, at its foot, he set out; but the god made it-self a snake and tried to bar the way. The prince, in one leap, was past it; but the sky grew dark at once, and he lost his path, grew faint and fell. He saw a spring near by, though; and when he had had a drink he could hold up his head. He had his men take him to Ot-su in I-se, where he found at the foot of a pine tree the sword he had laid off when he went to put down the god. He was still weak, but he took great care to make gifts to the god-dess at I-se, to tell all he had seen and done in the three years he had been gone, and to pray and give thanks that he had come through it all with his life. Then he sent word to his sire of what he had done, told him that he was nigh to death and would like to see him; but he died ere this could be. His corpse was laid at No-bo-no in I-se. The tale says that a white bird flew up from his tomb, in which there was naught left but the wreath and grave robes of the brave prince. The bird, it is said, flew to the Plain of the Ko-lo Play-e-res in Ya-ma-to, which from that time has been known as Mi-sa-za-ka Shi-ra-to-ri, or Im-pe-ri-al Tomb of the White Bird. That was in the year 113 A. D. Ya-ma-to was then thir-ty-six years old, and since that time shrines have been set up to him in most all parts of Ja-pan, and to this day folks pray to him as a god.

CHAPTER V.

JAPAN'S FIRST FOREIGN CONQUEST.

The Mi-ka-do Se-i-mu took the place of old Ke-i-ko, whose son Ya-ma-to-Da-ke had been dead most a score of years, ere his soul went to join that of the brave prince. When Se-i-mu's reign of six-ty years was done, Chi-na-i took his place, and he was the spouse of the great Em-press Jin-gu Ko-go, who led the most grand war told of in the tales of Ja-pan since the first great feat of Jim-mu.

Jin-gu was fair to look at, good, quick of mind, strong and brave. She paid great heed to the gods, and they, the Jap-a-nese would tell you, chose her out of all the good folks of the realm to be the one who should hear their will and know their plans for the good of the realm. They told her what great things the Jap-a-nese might do, and she had the faith to go where they said, and a bold, brave heart that knew no fear on sea or land, in peace or war.

In the first year of her lord's reign there was an out-break of some of the tribes in Ku-ma-so, a part of Ki-u-shi-u, and Chi-u-ai at the head of his troops went down to make peace, while his wife and some of his folks came on in ships. Jin-gu's heart was full of hope that they might win in this war, and by it join all the Ku-ma-so folks to their throne. She went to pray on one of the isles of the In-land Sea, and while at her shrine one of the gods spoke to her and said, "Why do you wish so much to gain sway in Ku-ma-so? That is but a poor place, not worth the cost of this great war you would make. But there is a rich land, sweet and fair, bright with gold and ores, and gems of all sorts that have much worth; it lies in Shi-ra-ki" (that is Co-re-a), "and if you pray and make gifts to me, and keep your thoughts on me, I will lead you to that land and will give it in-to your hands, yet cause you to shed no blood; and I will give you sway in Ku-ma-so as well." Jin-gu told this to her spouse, but he did not share her faith that it was words come to them from the gods. He went up to the top of a great hill, from which he could see far to the West; but as all sea and no land met his view he said, "I see no new lands; if there is not some in the sky, then you tell me what is not true. My sires paid their court to all the gods; is there an-y to whom they did not pray and make gifts?" The gods, through Jin-gu, sent word that if the Mi-ka-do had doubts, and thought that what they said was not true, then they would not aid Chi-u-ai; but his good wife should go to the new land and her-self win all its wealth. But Chi-u-ai went on in his war with the folks of Ku-ma-so, and they beat him. Then, while in camp, he fell sick and died. But the troops were not told of his death, and the brave Jin-gu, with the Mi-ka-do's chief man of state, went on with the strife till they won the field. Then the brave em-press thought of the realm of

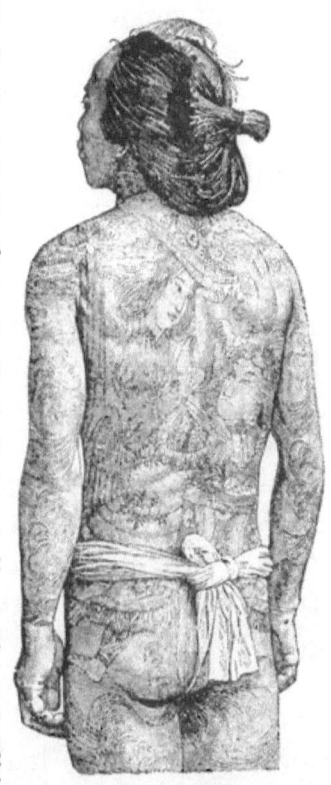

TAT-TOOED MAN.

the West which the gods had told her of; and when she had tried some tests to see if her course were right, and found that the gods were still with her, she set out to cross that great stretch of strange sea, which is so broad that she could find no trace of the land that bounds it on the West. It was a great task to make up all the troop and to build all the ships she would need. But she had no fear of great tasks. She sought the aid of her chief men-at-arms, whom she said she would lead, in the guise of a man. If her scheme should fail she would take all the blame; but if it did not, the praise should be theirs. The men swore that they would stand by her and go where she led, to the end. They set to work; troops were brought in from all parts of the realm, and at last, when Jin-gu had gone through her last rites to the gods, and had made her last charge to her men as to how they should act in the new land, and to the new folks they were to meet, they set out with this word from the god, who had led her to take this bold step: "The Spir-it of Peace will at all times guide you and take care of your life. The Spir-it of War will go on in front of you and lead your ships." The brave em-press, as well as her sea-men, did not know just where Co-re-a lies; they had no chart and no com-pass, but with the sun, stars and the flights of birds as the guides meant by the gods, and with winds, waves and tides right to aid them, they made a quick and safe trip, and brought their ships to beach in the south part of Co-re-a. It was a fine, bright day, and the sun shone on the arms of the host, as rank on rank they set foot on the shore, till they made such a grand show that the Co-re-ans were struck with fear and awe. The king of this part of the realm, who had been told that a strange fleet from the East was in sight, felt the same as his folks,

A WREST-LING CIR-CUS.

and cried out: "We did not know that there was a land out-side of ours. Have our gods left us?" It seems as if he did not think he could drive the Jap-a-nese out, but at once sent his men to meet them with a white flag borne on high, to show that they meant peace. The two bands met on good terms, and Jin-gu had been but a short time in this strange land when its folks gave them-selves and their wealth up to her, and made an oath that they would own the head of Ja-pan as their great chief, that they would send some of their wealth to this chief from time to time, and some of their best men, too, that the Jap-a-nese might be sure that they still held to their oath and have no cause to come with their troops on an-y more such trips as this one. Streams might flow back-ward, they said, or the small stones in their beds leap up to the stars, yet they would not break their oath. So Jin-gu said she would not make war, and the king had four-score of the ships well stored with gold and silks, and wealth of all kinds; and four-score men of high rank were put on board as his pledge of good faith. With these Jin-gu and her vast host went back to Ja-pan. They had been gone but two months, and in that time had done the most grand thing in all their his-to-ry — a feat more great than the war of Jim-mu, for with all that she had done no blood had been shed and no life lost. It was the first time the Jap-a-nese had gone to a strange land to fight, and to this day they take great pride in it, and tell how they first made "the arms of Ja-pan shine be-yond the seas."

When Jin-gu got home she had a son whom the Jap-a-nese look on as the god of war. Then the

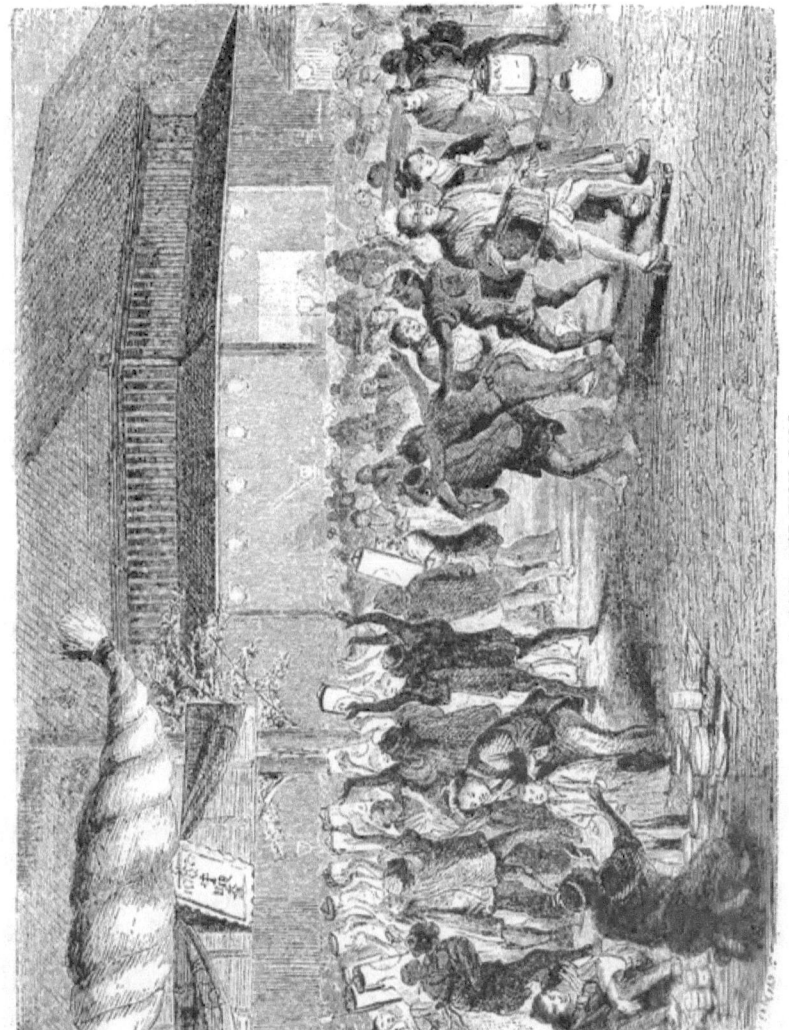

A RICE AUCTION SALE.

death of Chi-u-ai was made known, and in due form the em-press went through the rites of the dead ere she made her way back to her court. This was in the eight hun-dred and six-ty-third year of the Jap-a-nese em-pire, or as we count the years 203 A. D. Jin-gu kept the throne for near three score and ten years more. It was a reign in which much new thought and new ways of life came to the realm from the Co-re-ans, who got their ways from the Chi-nese, but of whom the Jap-a-nese had not heard ere this. Then, too, Jin-gu made a great change in the plan on which the em-pire was laid out. The Mi-ka-do who held the throne ere Chi-u-ai's time, had cut it up a-new from the old, rough plan of the fiefs that were held by the sho-guns, which Su-jin laid out in the year 25 A. D.; but now Jin-gu made a new plan, like that in Co-re-a, with five home states, in which was the chief town and the seat of the court, and sev-en more states, or *do* as the Jap-a-nese call them, whose names show which way they lie from the seat of the em-pire. This form, for the most part, has been kept till now, though in those days the folks knew much less of the size and shape of the isles that make up their realm, than they do now. All parts were known by these *do* names, and there were not, as we might think, names for each of the isles by it-self. In fact, it was not till a long time that they came to know that the main isle, Hou-do, was an isle. If you should hear folks call this main isle Nip-pon, you may be sure that they do not know the Jap-a-nese well, for to them that name stands for the whole land.

Jin-gu, and her son, O-jin, are now great gods in

A TOMB.

the Shin-to. There are a host of shrines to them in all parts of the realm, and men of arms and men of the sea pray to O-jin as the god of war, like Mars was to the Greeks in days of old; and boys are taught to look to Jin-gu and to think of her life and brave deeds, as if she were a man in whose steps they must try to tread. She is put with the great men, not the wom-en, when on the 5th of May each year the pic-tures, dolls and fig-ures of the house are brought out and the youths are told tales of those sires who have done grand things for the ho-ly realm of Dai (great) Nip-pon, and are taught that they must try to be as great and good as their sires.

It was a tide of new life that this great queen brought to her realm when she made Co-re-ans take an oath to send her of their wealth and their men as a pledge of their faith to her. For five cent-u-ries—from the 3d to the 8th—this new stream of life bore on its flood a great load from A-si-a to Ja-pan of all those things which make folks more fine and less rude, and give them a taste for what things are good, and pure and high, in place of wild ways, strife and war—that is, it gave the Jap-a-nese a love for books and taught them how to write. It gave them a new faith, which did much to change and raise the Shin-to, but did not wipe it out. It taught them how to think and gave them new views of life. It told them of laws, of how to heal the sick, of more of sci-ence, and gave them much new light on art. Folks from the West came to live in the land, who could teach the Jap-a-nese how to use their hands as well as their minds in ways they knew naught of ere this. Though this great change took its start in Jin-gu's time, there are few tales told of who came to Ja-pan from Co-re-a in her reign. In her son's day we read of some three hun-dred tail-ors who came, and most three hun-dred fine steeds that were sent as a gift from the king; and it was then, too, that a man who had read books a great deal, and was well learnt, came to dwell at the Court for a while and taught the Mi-ka-do's son how to write. Quite a long time went by, though, ere much use was made of this new art by the Jap-a-nese, and it was not till 403 A. D., that there was an-y one kept at court to make note of what took place in the realm. Near this time some mul-ber-ry trees were brought from the West and set out, and the care of silk-worms came to be known here as in Chi-na and Co-re-a. The two realms seem to have been on the best of terms, for some of the Co-re-ans who went there must have gone of their own will. There were great bands of work-men, trades-men and plain folks of all crafts who went from Co-re-a to make them-selves at home in the strange isles of the East. Ja-pan must have thought a great deal of her new realm, too, for she used it well, and once when the food gave out there the Mi-ka-do sent vast loads of grain to the poor folks. In the year 552 there came to the sea-girt em-pire as friends some men from the Court of Chi-na, as well as quite a band of Co-re-ans, some of whom had great gifts in sci-ence and art, and some who were priests of Bud-dha. This was the great faith of the lands west of Ja-pan, and was not at all like the rude Shin-to. It soon spread till it got a strong hold on the folks, rich as well as poor, and for years it has been the chief faith of most of the Jap-a-nese, as it is of near one-third of all the folks on the globe.

CHAPTER VI.

HOW JAPAN FELL UNDER MILITARY RULE.

For near six hun-dred years from the time of Jin-gu not much is known of what took place in this realm of the far East. There is a long list of the Mi-ka-dos who held the throne, with now and then a few notes of what they did with Co-re-a and Chi-na. But in the course of that long time we know that the faith of Bud-dha and some of the Chi-nese modes of rule got firm root in the land. Some one has said that these brought to an end the Gold-en Age of the Mi-ka-dos' sway. Ere long the

Em-per-or and his chief man of state took the new faith and a vast change was wrought in the realm. For one thing, it broke up the long reigns that had been one great cause of the strength of the throne, and in more ways than one it made the Mi-ka-do

A NO-BLE SEN-TENCED TO THE HA-RI KA-RI.

lose part of his hold on the folks, and led to a new sort of rule. In the eighth cent-u-ry the court did a great deal to spread this faith. The men whose place it was to wait on the Mi-ka-do were full of zeal to do all that the creed calls for and to be well learnt in the ho-ly books of In-di-a. Word was sent out that two great shrines and a tall church—which is known as a pa-go-da—sev-en sto-ries high, should be built in each fief of the realm. The ranks of the priests grew to great size, and there were scores of homes built for those men who had a wish to be monks and for the rest of their lives to read the Bud-dhist books and live for naught but their faith. The em-per-ors, and the em-press-es, too, thought much of how they might spread this new faith through their whole realm, and it soon came to be the way with the Mi-ka-dos to leave the throne when they had held it for a few years and turn monks. They would shave their heads, as a sign that they were to have no more to do with the world, and would take the name of Ho-o, which means the Em-per-or-Monk of Bud-dha. The Mi-ka-do who took the place of O-jin had a long reign, but that of the next one was short; and so it went on for a long time. When a mi-ka-do had held the throne for a year or so, he would leave it to his son, who might be but a year or two old, and this boy would do the same, so that the realm was in the hands of the chief monks, the men of state, of the court, and not in the sway of the throne at all. Of course this was bad for the rule and for the folks who could not look up to their Mi-ka-do as those of old had done to the brave men-at-arms and the kings of firm will and wise minds, strong frames and good health, who had led their troops in great wars and had had the good and the growth of all parts of their realm at heart. But while the race on the throne grew weak, the class that bore arms (which, as we know, was made to have a good deal of sway in the days of the first mi-ka-dos) grew more strong, and at last they made a great change in the form of rule in the Jap-a-nese Em-pire.

From the time that Jin-gu's war had let the flood of life come in from the West, more than one change had crept in, which in a still way brought forth a new state of things in the whole land, in the course of time. But the two things that did more than aught else to mold the life of the Jap-a-nese in-to what the rest of the world found it less than a score of years a-go were Bud-dhism and Feu-dal-ism. The new faith, which came first, led a large part of the folks to give up their old gods, or look at them in a new light; to change in part their aims in life, their ways, and e-ven their food; and more than this, its priests brought to the realm the germs of new arts and taught the folks to read, write and speak the tongue of Chi-na, and made known to them not a few new kinds of work, which the quick minds of the Jap-a-nese soon made their own, and wrought out with such skill as is seen in no place else. The work of Bud-dhism was to mold the minds and ways of the folks; that of Feu-dal-ism was to put the realm in the rule of the Sho-guns and to cut it up in-to fiefs, in each of which a Dai-mi-o or chief held sway like a king. His life was spent to gain lands and win in wars, his home was a vast fort, in the chief town of the fief, with stout walls, through which no strange man could go till he had shown he had a right to, and his house-hold was like a small town of men-at-arms, who kept guard for their lord in peace and fought for him in war.

In this the Mid-dle A-ges of Ja-pan were like those of Eu-rope, in both of which Feu-dal-ism rose at the same time, though when it came to an end in the fif-teenth cent-u-ry in Eu-rope, it was just on the rise to its height in Ja-pan, where it was brought to a more high state than in an-y land of the East.

For a long time ere this class rose to an-y great strength, the realm was for the most part in the hands of some lords of high rank, who did not bear arms. From them the knights of the field made up their minds to get the reins of rule. These were the Ku-ge or court lords of the proud Fu-ji-wa-ra

A THE-A-TER IN YED-DO.

stock, the first great race in Ja-pan, which was not of the Mi-ka-do's house. They said they came from Am-e, who served the grand-sire of Jim-mu. The first great lord of this house, by some means, rose with the folks at Court till he came to be Ku-am-ba-ku, or Re-gent, for one of the young mi-ka-dos; and to take this post, which was the most high that an-y sub-ject could hold, came to be the right of his race. From this house sprung the chief lords of the realm. At first they held chief rank in arms as well as at Court, but ere long they grew so fond of ease that they left the fame and spoils of war to be won by those who would fight for them, while they gave them-selves up to life at Court, where they had full sway and rank next to the Mi-ka-do's own house. They made them-selves a bar to cut the Mi-ka-do off from the mass of his folks. As time went on the gulf grew to be still more wide, till at last he was like a man that did not dwell in the same realm with them at all. He was not seen by an-y one but his wife, the folks of his own house, and a few of his most high men of state. He sat on a throne of mats, with a screen in front of him, and his feet did not touch the earth at an-y time, and when he rode out he was shut in from the view of the folks of the street. Thus, while his sway with the folks grew weak, that of the Fu-ji-wa-ra grew strong, till at last these lords got a great deal of the rule of the realm in their own hands. They put them-selves in the chief posts of trust and strength, and ere long did with the Em-pire as they chose, and made use of the young mi-ka-dos, who were mere boys, as tools to do their will.

The throne lost its rights so far that when a mi-ka-do had a wish to have an-y real sway in his realm, he would find he could gain it more as a monk than as the em-per-or on the throne. But for the most part the rule was in the hands of this proud race, till the Tai-ra took it from them by might at arms. For a thou-sand years, from the time of the brave Queen Jin-ju, till the great home war of the twelfth cent-u-ry—the worst in all her his-to-ry—the tale of Ja-pan is made up less of the deeds of the mi-ka-dos or of the realm in his hands, than of the feuds and fights of these lords and their kins-men, who were high born, rich, and some of them of grand and brave deeds; for the class that bore the arms of the Em-pire and fought her wars did not long let the Ku-gi class have the best of things at home. So much the more could they fight their own wars.

The em-per-ors them-selves were not all good men. One whose name was Bu-ret-su, and who had quite a long reign for those times in the last of the fifth cent-u-ry, and the first of the next, is said to have been hard and fond of coarse sports, like the Ro-man em-per-or Ne-ro. He would make his folks go up trees that he might fire on them and kill them, and he thought it great sport to catch folks and kill them when they did not know he was near. In the time of Bi-dat-su, who took the throne near four-score years af-ter the time of the Jap-a-nese Ne-ro, quite a bad war was led on the Bud-dhists by a man whose name was Mo-ri-a. He tore down the ho-ly things from their shrines, and burnt not a few of the shrines; but the strife was put down in the reign of the next mi-ka-do, and Mo-ri-a was slain. But peace was still far off, for the ranks of the men-at-arms were large and strong in these days, and war was their joy as well as their work in life. If they did not have it at home they made it somewhere else. In the reign of Ten-shi, near a hundred years from Mo-ri-a's war, a great host in a large fleet went to Co-re-a, where they made the king leave his throne and the folks own the Mi-ka-do of Ja-pan as their chief. But they did not meet with as good luck as this, when—in the same reign—they went to Chi-na. Thus the tale of the Realm of the Isles goes on till the great war of the twelfth cent-ur-y, when the Bu-ke (or knights at arms) of the house of He or Tai-ra, and the house of Gen or Min-a-mo-to, fell out in a great strife and brought on the worst home-war Ja-pan has known. It was the Ta-i-ra clan, led by Ki-o-mo-ri, who won in this war, and he was the first sho-gun, or gen-er-al, as we would say, who got the might of the throne out of the hands of the Mi-ka-do—or his Re-gent of Fu-ji-wa-ra blood—and made that great change in the form of rule by which ere long the em-per-or came to stand at the head of the realm in naught but name, and as the chief of all priests and monks in the faith, while some chief-at-arms, in the post of Great Sho-gun, was at the head of the state as

RE-CEP-TION DRESS.

well as of all the troops, and had charge of the realm in peace as much as in war.

The great strife and the change of rule that marks

this time as one of much note in the past of Ja-pan, came to pass in this way. As the Mi-ka-do's sway had grown weak and the Hu-ge and the Bu-ke had grown more strong, each came to have a great deal of ill-will for the oth-er, for each had a wish to be first in the realm and to get the Mi-ka-do in its own hands. And this ill-will grew and grew till at last it broke out in a great feud and threw all the realm in-to dread and strife. As long as the Gen and Ta-i-ra kept to war, the Fu-ji-wa-ra had naught to dread from them, and saw them grow great in their fame with no fear; but there were times of peace now and then when the bold, brave gen-er-als had time to see how the men who ruled the realm they fought for, took their ease and dwelt in wealth and peace. They had no such good things, but it was not long ere they made up their minds that they would like them as much as the Fu-ji-wa-ra. So they went to live at Ki-o-to, the chief town of the realm and the place where the court was held, and where all the great and rich lords dwelt. At the same time the Ku-ge saw that if they did not take care, the fame these chiefs won in the wars would raise them too high in the state. Now the court (which had no might at arms it-self) was most glad to have the chiefs put an end to these brawls when they rose. But the court lords did not like it at all when there came to be signs that the Bu-ke would be as great as they. Their first step to check this, was to make a rule that the court should not give high rank to an-y Ta-i-ra or Gen, let his claims be what they might; then they sent word that the bands of self-made men-at-arms, which had spread through a large part of the realm in the past few years, must not join the ranks of these sho-guns; but this did not do much good, for the men did as they chose, and they did not choose to leave chiefs who paid them so well, and of whom they had grown so fond. Then they tried to set one clan to check the oth-er, and that, too, did not work well. But if they could not make an-y one else serve mean tricks on these great sho-guns, they did it themselves. When the Gen clan brought all the North of Hon-du in-to the em-pire, and for most a score of years kept the whole of the Ku-an-to in peace, and went so far as to pay costs that the realm should have borne from their own funds, they made the court take no note of it at all; and when the chiefs asked for some gifts or pay for the men in the ranks, who had fought for all this, the Ku-ge sent no word back at all, and would not so much as let the Mi-ka-do own what they had done in his name, but spoke of the whole thing as some feuds of their own. So the Gen and the Ta-i-ra chiefs took it on them-selves to give grants of land to their men, and thus most of the men-at-arms grew to feel still more bound to their sho-guns and to think still less of the Court.

Step by step the Gen clan, which was the more strong of the two, got hold of some of the posts of note in the rule of the state; and all might have still gone well if these two great clans could have kept on good terms; but the house of Gen could not bear to see the men of Ta-i-ra rise in fame, and the Ta-i-ra, just as bad, felt a pang each time they saw a Gen gain a jot in name, or rank, or wealth. At last a cause was found to bring them to strife—which was the claims of two prin-ces to the throne. It was clear then that the side which won and made its prince the Mi-ka-do, would hold first rank in his realm; and they fought in a long hard strife for the prize. The chief who led the side that won at last, was Ki-o Mo-ri of the Ta-i-ra race. He was a young man who had been full of fire and life, and thirst for fame from the time he was a small boy. He had been bred to arms, and ere he was a score of years old he had made a cruise of much note to get hold of some sea thieves that had done a great deal to vex the Jap-a-nese. Part of his life was spent at Ki-o-to and part in the field of war at the South, so he knew the ways of town and court, as well as of war, when the time came for him to take the place of his sire as one of the chief men of state. It was in the same year that the two prin-ces laid claim to the throne, and the house of Ta-i-ra took sides with Ki-o Mo-ri while his foe had the aid of the Gen or Min-a-mo-to clan. It was in a way, like England's war of the Ro-ses; the Ta-i-ra with their red flags, and the Gen with their white, fought hard each for its own prince. The Ta-i-ra won, for they got the house of the em-per-or out of the hands of all the rest, and their prince was put on the throne; and from then till now no one in the realm has had so much sway as the head of the set on the side of the Mi-ka-do. Ki-o Mo-ri now had the rule of all Ja-pan in his own grasp; for the Mi-ka-do knew it was through him

OF-FI-CER IN COURT DRESS.

that he had the throne, so he gave him his way in all things—as he could not help but do.

Ki-o Mo-ri let no chance go by to raise him-self and his house; and at last he held a place in the realm at the head of all the rest of the great men of state, and the sons of his race were in most of the best posts, both at court and in arms. And he, too, kept his place in the guard at arms. This is how the house of Ta-i-ra came to be the most strong in the realm—and more strong than the Fu-ji-wa-ra had been. This is how, too, that the sho-guns and the rest of the class that in times past had had no place but on the field of war, now came to have the whole of the realm in their hands. It was the first of what is known as the mil-i-ta-ry rule—which brought great change to Ja-pan, and was kept up for sev-en hun-dred years; for it fell but a score of years a-go. Ki-o Mo-ri was at the head of all the Jap-a-nese troops, and ere long he was in all but name the em-per-or of the realm; he had rid him-self of all his foes in court and out of it; he and three-score of his kins-men held most of the high posts in the realm; they had great wealth, for the tax of more than thir-ty fiefs went to them; they built grand homes in Ki-o-to and else-where, and at last he made two of his sons sho-guns of first rank, and his girl-child the wife of the boy Mi-ka-do then on

A DRUG SHOP AT YED-DO.

the throne. The Fu-ji-wa-ra had no might at arms, and were, by the rise of the Ta-i-ra, put in the shade for all time; and Ki-o Mo-ri did not rest till he had, as he thought, got all the Gen folks out of his way, so that through a long line the race of the Ta-i-ra might be the chiefs of the great Em-pire of the Rising Sun. But his wish did not come to pass.

CHAPTER VII.

THE RULE OF THE HOUSE OF GEN.

Though Ki-o Mo-ri had put to death the chief men of the house of Gen, lest they should rise up in their strength and drive him from the high place he had won, he had said he would spare the lives of two of the old chief's sons. The first one, from whom he had the most to fear, was dead, he thought, and the young ones were sent to live with some Bud-dhist monks and grow up to be priests. But Ki-o Mo-ri should have known that these boys had the hot blood of their brave sires in their veins, and since he had been so bad as to kill them, he should have done the same to their sons if it was his wish to keep all he had won for his own race.

The first son, Yo-ri-to-mo, had got off with his life, as well as the two young ones, though he was in the last fight which his sire lost and had the ill luck to fall in the hands of one of the Ta-i-ra men. But through the aid of some folks who felt for the boy, he was not put to death, but was sent to live far off in the fief of Id-zu, in the care of two Ta-i-ra men. He had the gifts of a great man; his will was strong, his heart brave; he knew how to feel joy, grief or wrath and not show them in his face; he could bear a great deal, as he had to both in the fall of his race and in the ills of war. At the same time he won the love and best will of those he was with. So when the proud, hard ways of Ki-o Mo-ri got to such a pitch that a prince of the blood made up his mind to rid the realm of him if he had to put him to death, this prince knew that Yo-ri-to-mo and the Gen clan would be just the men to help him. He wrote to Yo-ri-to-mo, and he in turn wrote to his bold young broth-er, Yosh-it-su-ne, and to his friends, to join him and take up arms to put down the old foe of their race.

Now there was not in all the isles of the realm a knight more great and good than this Yosh-it-su-ne. He was not so old as his broth-er by twelve years, but he was, as we say, the "flow-er of his age." He had been put with his small broth-er to live with the monks when his sire was put to death, but he had too much love for life and sports, and was too true a son of the Sho-gun, to want to spend his years with books; so one day he ran off from the monks' house with some man of trade who had come from the East to sell steel to the folks who dwelt near the monks. The man did not want to take him, but the boy would go, and they soon came to be warm friends. On their way they made a stop at Kad-zu-sa, which was then a prey to a band of thieves, with whom Yosh-it-su-ne had some fights and did such bold deeds to drive them out that his friend had to beg him not to put forth his strength too much or the Ta-i-ra would hear of it and know at once from what race he came; and that would be the end of him. So the young man kept as still as he could and went on with his friend to Mut-su, where he went to live with a prince of the old Fu-ji-wa-ra house. He spent his time in the chase, in the sports of which he was fond, and in drill at arms; and in the mean-time he grew to be strong and brave, and in all things the type of a Jap-a-nese knight. When the call came to him from Yo-ri-to-mo he went to the field at once, and the grand fight that he made for the pride of his race did more

The Rule of the House of Gen.

to place the house of Gen at the head of the state and to drive out the Ta-i-ra than all the spread of Yo-ri-to-mo, though he got the place of chief and most of the spoils. In the first of this fight, when the Ta-i-ra race and the house of Gen met in strife once more, the Ta-i-ra beat Yo-ri-to-mo and he had to flee for his life. But he found a new band that would let him lead them, and ere long he made up a large force from the folks who had once been led by his sires, but who till now had held back in fear of the might of the Ta-i-ra sway. Like the true Jap-a-nese Sho-gun that he was, when he found the folks glad to join with him, he lost no time ere he had made up a large force and got them all in fine

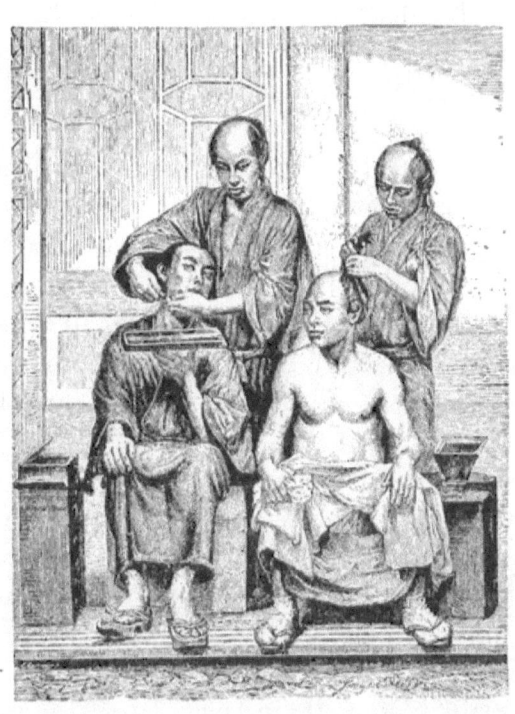

BAR-BERS.

shape for war. He woke his clan up to new life, and drew to his side not a few of the men who had lost their love for the Ta-i-ra or had found their schemes at Court to fail, and would now put forth all the might they had to push on the plans of their great arch-foe. In the mean-time Ki-o Mo-ri had been at work and had got up a large force which was sent to the East just in time to get to one side of the Fu-ji Riv-er just as Yo-ri-to-mo came up to the oth-er. But this is the most swift of all the streams in Ja-pan, and though both troops had a great wish to meet and fight, they could not cross the flood. At last the Ta-i-ra took fright and fled in haste, sure that the Gen were at their heels, while they, for their part, soon went back to Ka-ma-ku-ra, where Yo-ri-to-mo set out to build a great town that in time came to be more grand in size and wealth and to have more sway in Ja-pan than old and great Ki-o-to it-self. He now made it his work to build up the might of this town and fix the sway of the Gen house here, and to wipe out the name of Ta-i-ra from the face of the earth. In the mean-time his broth-er and brave kins-folk led the hosts in the fierce war which soon spread through the whole realm. Ere long Ki-o Mo-ri fell sick and died at Ki-o-to, and his son took his place at the head of the house of Ta-i-ra; but the star of that race was now on its down-ward course, for the Gen troops won in the East, in the North, and the West, and at last they got Ki-o-to it-self, the chief town, the seat of the court and state, in their hands. The Ta-i-ra, the young Mi-ka-do, his folks and near friends, had to flee, while his broth-er was put on the throne and the wealth of the proud Ta-i-ra went to the chief who had sent them forth. Yosh-it-zu-ne, then the first man-at-arms of

PUN-ISH-MENTS.

the whole realm, went so far as to lay siege to the forts where the Ta-i-ra had tried to set up their strength and to plan means by which to get back what they had lost; and he drove them from place to place till at last they were on the sea, where each had a fleet of junks that met in a great fray that was to bring the dread war to an end. Though the Gen had all the odds in this fray, the Ta-i-ra fought best, and would have won if one of their men had not been false to them and lent aid to Yosh-it-zu-ne. It was a fierce fight to the end, and the day was not won till there was scarce a child of the Ta-i-ra left in all the fleet. Then all that were on land were sought out and put to death ere their foes felt free to be gay o-ver the great things they had done and the way they had paid off to the race of Ki-o Mo-ri the score he had left them when he slew their sire to make way for his own rise.

While this dread strife went on Yo-ri-to-mo's great task was to build up his strength and sway at Ka-ma-ku-ra, and to keep on in his plans till he had the whole of the real rule of the land in his hands. So it came round that Ja-pan at last was un-der two-fold form of rule. The Mi-ka-do, at Ki-o-to, was still the Em-per-or, and held his court as the great head of the realm. Though no one else had such a thought as to take the throne, his reign was not his rule; while the great Sho-gun, who still had to own the Mi-ka-do as his chief, had the reins of rule. He had a seat and sort of court of his own, three hun-dred miles from that of the Mi-ka-do's. He made more than one change in the state, chief of which was to form a coun-cil, which saw to the ways and needs of the realm. He set up a court, too, which tried all who did an-y crime, most of all the thieves (of which there were then great bands in Ja-pan). Scores of new ways to deal with the folks were laid out and brought up to the Mi-ka-do, who let them be put in force in his name, though some of them were far from the old forms of his sires, and not just what he would have done him-self. In this way Yo-ri-to-mo got the roy-al word to wipe out the Ta-i-ra house from all the posts of trust, and to put his own

PUN-ISH-MENTS.

kin in their stead. He took arms and all tools of war from the monks, too. They had come to have great stores of this sort, and could use them with much skill, so that when they felt they had cause to fight they could oft send out as fine a set of troops as was kept by the state in an-y part of the realm. They had wealth, too, and so far lost sight of the aim they laid claims to in life, that they kept them-selves like sets of real troops, in trim to break forth an-y day and fight the cause of an-y side they chose to take. This was not good for the realm, and Yo-ri-to-mo soon broke it up. Thus, step by step, he got more rights from the throne and brought things round to suit him-self, till at last he had a sure place as the head of the realm.

In five great fiefs sho-guns were put in charge, where there had been gov-ern-ors of the civ-il class; in the small fiefs, the civ-il gov-ern-ors were made to share their posts with (or to yield them in all but name) to chiefs-at-arms of the Gen race; and in all parts of the realm a tax was laid on to keep them in troops, so that a good force might be on hand at all times, and there would be no need to call out the troops of the East when small feuds broke out in strife. Ere long he sent folks to live in the lands of the North and the East which had been made to own the sway of the Mi-ka-do and pay tax to him. Soon those lands were made a part of the realm, with the same form of rule as the rest. Still more lands at the North did he add, and from the year 1180 on he had more might than an-y man in the em-pire, e-ven the Mi-ka-do him-self, and all the lords of the court paid to him the most high hon-ors that were known to them. In that year he made a vis-it to the Mi-ka-do and when he went back to Ka-ma-ku-ra, it was with more sway in the state than the old Fu-ji-wa-ra had held at an-y time, and more might at arms than the

PLOW-ING AND SOW-ING A RICE FIELD.

great house of Ta-i-ra had known. In a few years he was made Sei-i Ta-i Sho-gun, or Great Gen-er-al,

AT WORK IN A RICE FIELD.

which was a rank that had not been known in Ja-pan ere this, but which was kept up till 1868. From that time it meant much more to be a sho-gun than it had in the past; it meant so much that folks who went to Ja-pan from strange lands, thought that there were two heads of the em-pire. But that was not so. Great as was the Sho-gun's rule, it was at all times in the name of his lord, the Mi-ka-do at Ki-o-to.

With this last rise of Yo-ri-to-mo peace came to Ja-pan, and the great Gen-er-al spent the prime of his life in plans to make his rule sound and sure, and to have his sons and all his race brave and strong, so that they could hold the place he had made for them through all the years to come.

But there is one blot of his fair name. So long as he could use men for his own aims he was good to them, but as soon as he thought they might come to be great in them-selves, in fear that they might rise to out-shine him, he got them out of the way; and most of all he did this with his good broth-er Yosh-it-zu-ne, who, in truth, won more for Yo-ri-to-mo than the great Sho-gun did for him-self, but who won so much love from all folks as well as such great fame by his deeds in war, that his broth-er came to fear lest he should rise too high, and then to hate him, and at last to give word to have him put to death. But though Yo-ri-to-mo got all that he tried to, and more, and ranks as one of the first

GRAND TEM-PLE.

of all Ja-pan's great men in the state and in arms, it is not he, but Yosh-it-zu-ne, whose name is now held most high, whose place is thought to be with the gods, and to whom the folks have built shrines and pray. The young folks are told the tale of his life and his great deeds ; his face is on their kites ; and they all think of him as the type of what a true Jap-a-nese knight should be. Yo-ri-to-mo spent his life to serve him-self, and when he died his rule fell, his town was burnt to the ground, and he was put in his grave with few to think of him in time to come. But his young broth-er's fame still lives, and the boys of Ja-pan are still taught to be good and brave, and to have high aims in their lives as this knight of old had in his.

CHAPTER VIII.

THE WAYS OF WAR IN FEUDAL TIMES.

It was in Yo-ri-to-mo's day that feu-dal-ism spread it-self through most all parts of the realm. It got its start back near the close of the eighth cent-u-ry, when the Court made the plan to have a force of home ranks in each part of the realm, and to raise such a host of new troops had said that all those of the rich farm folks who were strong and smart, and who knew how to use the bow and ride a horse well should bear arms, and form a new class, known as the Sam-u-rai, while the rest who were weak of mind or limb should keep on and till the soil. And, more than that, it was said that there

MAK-ING BRIDG-ES.

should be naught to keep an-y of these Sam-u-rai who fought well and bore them-selves like true knights, from the most high posts that a man-at-arms could hold. Thus there was a prize in view for each of these farm-born guards, and not a few of them soon won a place and high rank in their troops. But ere a plain man like this could be put in charge of the Mi-ka-do's troops, he must needs go to Ki-o-to to serve as a court page, wait on some great lord or fill some place where he could learn how things were done in the name of the throne.

But they learnt more than that at Court; they learnt how court folks did for them-selves at Ki-o-to; they saw the strife for rank and fame that went on all the time with the lords great and small; and when they went back to their homes, their minds were full of plans to do the same thing in a small way. The folks where they dwelt were sure to think more of them for their stay at Ki-o-to and all they must have learnt of the ways at court, than of those who had not been to town; and so they oft came to rule quite large parts of the fiefs in which they dwelt. When they were sent for at Ki-o-to they would not go; nor did the Ku-ge Gov-ern-ors of the fiefs dare to do aught to them, for they had arms and steeds and men in their train to make up a good strong band for fray. In this way a large class grew up and spread through Ja-pan who called them-selves men-at-arms (though they would serve an-y great chief for pay) and who did a great deal to help on small feuds and clan-fights which were apt to spread till the whole fief was in a brawl; and the Court would have to send out a force in charge of a Ta-i-ra or Gen chief to check the strife. Now these chiefs, or sho-guns, would not make up all their force from the ranks of the realm but would get the aid of some such bands as those he was sent to quell who were not yet in the brawl, but were at all times glad to take part in a fray if they knew they would be well paid for it.

Thus you see these men who took up arms in their own right grew more strong and not less so, as would have been best for the Court rule; and, as time went on, there grew to be ties that bound the men in clans to this or that chief for whom they fought, so that they would not leave him for an-y thing.

In the mean-time the folks came to feel more and more that the Court had lost its hold on them; and while they still thought of the Mi-ka-do as their great king, the Son of Heav-en, whose word was law and who owned them as his slaves, they did not serve him, but some "great name" or Dai-mi-o, as the Jap-a-nese say, in his stead. To the clan of some strong prince they would be bound for peace and war. They would fight his cause with glad hearts, and if he were slain, they would die, too. By their strength and zeal, he could soon claim the whole fief, and rule all folks as much as those who bore his arms. Those who worked the farms, kept shops or plied a trade, all came at last to be in the care of some chief to whose fort-like house they could flee in time of harm and whose band of brave men-at-arms was on hand at all times to do his will. And the tax — which was of so much rice — these folks did not pay to the realm, as had been their wont, but to their chiefs, who spent their wealth on their clans, on them-selves and their homes. The home of a Dai-mi-o, with its walls and moats, its vast courts and high tow-ers, was like a great fort, with-in which was a small town. At its gates there was a lodge, where a guard of armed men was kept at all times; and though a man from some oth-er clan might be made at home in all parts else of the great chief's house, he was not at an-y time let to go in-to the fort in-side where the Dai-mi-o's arms and wealth were kept. This was the rule with all clans. The Jap-a-nese knights, like those of the West, had a high sense of what was due their chief and right for them-selves, and a long code of rules, as to what was due them from both friend and foe and what they should do to both.

No man held so low a rank that by brave deeds and good faith to his chief he might not rise to a high place in charge of a large force, with a great name and much wealth; and when such a rise was made it was a grand time in the fort and through the whole fief. The Sam-u-rai, of which these knights were one class, have long been the most bright type of all the Jap-a-nese folks. They have done more than hold the fiefs and fight the wars of their clans; they were her first trav-el-ers and men of books and of arts. They—we are told—are the men

STREET IN YO-KO-HA-MA.

whose minds have been the best and the most quick to learn, and the most wise to act. It was of this class that the plan of feu-dal-ism was born; and it was they who broke it up, swept down the sho-gun rule in 1868, put the reins once more in the Mi-ka-do's hands and said, we will send our young men to the great West and will wake Ja-pan out of her past, and make her a realm of the new world. They were in the Mid-dle A-ges, as now, the soul of the realm. As they are now the best men in this new age of peace, they were the best chiefs, the best rank and file in the old days.

A Sam-u-rai, then, was not seen out of doors that he did not have his two swords—a long and a short one—at his belt. A guard was at the gate of his house—or his fort, if he was a great man—all the time; and on the porch, in front of his house, there were spears, both great and small; bows and darts, and more than one war-ax would be set on their butts to be at hand in case of need. In the halls were coats of mail and all the dress for war, as well as long spears, which the wom-en of the house knew how to use in case foes should come on the place when the men were not there.

The men-at-arms of those days bore shields and wore casques, and suits of mail, made of chain or of scales, some of iron, brass or steel, and some of shark-skin or the hide of beasts made hard. More stuffs than these were made use of some-times; for in their war-tools, as in all their home things, the Jap-a-nese made great use of lac-quer, a sort of fine, hard var-nish that they made from the gum of a tree and spread on met-als, on wood, on pa-per and a great ma-ny things to give them a hard sur-

A STATE DINNER.

face, as well as to make them smooth and brignt to look at.

The Jap-a-nese ranks were a fine sight to see when they set out for the field of war. Since the land was so much made up of hills and vales, or the wet plains where rice grew, they had small use for horse-men, and most of the troops were on foot. The race, you know, as a rule, is not so large as ours; but the men were straight and of good shape, bore their arms well and made a bright show with their suits of black, white, blue, green, gold and sil-ver mail, the gay cords that bound their sword hilts, and their grand crests, and the silk of their dress that could be seen here and there when there was a gap in the mail. They bore tall spears in their hands that caught the sun, and the casques of their chiefs were some-times as much as three feet tall. Drums, sticks of hard wood, with which to clap, and conch-shells, made up their band, and gave them the calls of the march, the camp, and the field.

The Jap-a-nese learnt ma-ny arts of war from the Chi-nese, through Co-re-a, but, as with all that they learnt from that land, they made much change in them to suit their own needs. For a time they would try one mode, then some new one, but at last, in the rule of the Ash-i-ka-ga, two men brought forth the best that had yet been tried ; and that was kept in use till the great change of late years, when the Jap-a-nese gave up their own modes of war-fare for those of Eu-rope.

In the field, a rain of darts from each side was most of the time the way a fray be-gan. Then there would be a fight the length of the whole line for a time till the strife grew so fierce that the ranks got in one great mob, where each man's sole thought was to cut off all the heads he could with his sword. It was not a rare thing for the chief of each side to come out in front

WIN-TER DRESS OF THE FISH-ER-MEN AND PEAS-ANTS.

of the ranks, and to spare their troops, end the strife by one hand-to-hand fight. When they met by chance in the great fray, it would be the same. Their men would slack their strife: they could give no aid to their chiefs, but had to stand to one side to watch the fight, and each band would call the name of their own man to cheer him on. The fight would rage till one of them had cut off the head of his foe. Then with the poor wretch's head held high in his hand, he would shout his name and yell it out that he had won the day. This would bring the strife to the same end as if the whole force of the foe had been cut down, and the clan of the chief who had won would shout their praise of his feat. Then those who had slain an-y foes of note had to pass in front of him and show him the heads they had cut off, at which he would give them such gifts as were thought meet for such brave deeds. If an-y had saved the life of the chief on the field, he was raised to a post of most high rank in the clan.

On the side that lost, those men who had been hurt would fall on their swords or kill them-selves in some way, so as not to fall in-to the hands of their foes; and an-y chief or man of note in the ranks would cut or flay his face so that it would not be known by the foes; for if they found it they would take great pride in it and put it in some place where scores of folks would see it and say how great was the man who could kill him. This was the right thing for all true knights to do in those days; and, more than that, there would be not a few of a chief's men who, though not hurt at all, would take their own lives; for it was not right, they thought, that they should live if their chief was slain.

When a force laid siege to a fort or a town, or the great house of some dai-mi-o, they built up in front of their camp a sort of screen of planks, with a steep slant. At the gates of these stood guards. A watch was kept on the hills, in high trees, or tow-ers built up for that use; and some-times huge kites that would hold a man were flown, and a bird's eye view was got of what lay with-in the walls of the foe. The facts thus learnt had much to do with the way the siege went on. Some-times the plan would be to starve them out; some-times to set fire to them, or shoot at them at long range; some-times feints of good-will would be made, or a ruse would be tried; and then, if all else were in vain, a charge would be made and the hosts would fall on the fort, smash in the gates, scale the walls, and take the place by storm and at the point of the sword, if the folks could not cut them down and drive them back ere they got so far.

The work of those who held the civ-il posts in the realm was not great in these days. They had to see that the folks were dealt with in just terms; that those who did wrong paid for their crimes; that no man took or had to give up more than his due. They had to hear both sides of no end of small feuds and set them at rest, and to take the tax from the folks at set times. This was quite a gay time with the farm folk. When the rice crops were well in, each man would put the share that he was to pay to the realm in straw bags and fix it in nice shape to go to the town where he must pay it. Then in fete dress him-self, and with his horse made gay with flaps and straps of red, a small bunch of bells here and there, he would put the rice bags on the beast and set off to pay his tax and have a good time with the friends he would be sure to meet on the road and at the end of the route.

CHAPTER IX.

THE WAYS OF PEACE IN FEU-DAL TIMES.

A REAL peace that spread through the whole realm and that they felt would last was not known to the Jap-a-nese till the time of I-ye-ya-su in the six-teenth cent-u-ry ; yet all through the long age of war there were times now and then, when no great strife shook the land and when the folks could think of the arts of peace, could work at crafts and give their minds to books and things that have naught to do with

RE-CEP-TION OF A HIGH FUNC-TION-A-RY.

war; and they came to do a great deal in these arts that the rest of the world looks at with awe for the skill and the taste that they see. As feu-dal-ism grew, so did Bud-dhism ; and with it there came from Chi-na a long list of arts and thoughts, crafts and trades, that were new to the Jap-a-nese, but which they soon took up and brought to a state that has not been known an-y-where else. And it was in Ki-o-to that this work, like all else in the life of the Jap-a-nese, got to its height. In the first part of feu-dal times this was the head of the Em-pire in all things; it was the seat of the Mi-ka-do and his Court and the chief sho-guns. There was the Guard of the Em-pire; there dwelt the high lords of the Ku-ge, and the chief priests of all sects of the Bud-dhist faith. It was the source from which went the streams that gave to the realm its faith, its thoughts and much of its work. There the chief tem-ples and homes for the monks were first built and may still be seen. It was the Ho-ly Cit-y for all the sects; and to it went priests and monks from far-off towns or way-side shrines, that they might, as they felt, drink from the stream of their faith, where it was near the source and pure. They would see the chief priests of their sect, pray at the great shrines, read the good books and be taught of the sage monks whom they felt to be close to the soul of Bud-dha—for you know it is taught in this faith that one goes through life ma-ny times, and each time in some new state, till at last he gets so pure that Bud-dha takes him to be a part of him-self, which is the height of bliss and the last stage of his life.

When a priest who had been in Ki-o-to went

back to his home, it was a great time for the whole place. The folks felt that he had drunk at the fount of life and would go in throngs to see him; while the priests of his own shrine heard him with awe, and gave place to him as to one more wise, more blest than them-selves.

To this great town the young men of high rank were sent from the most far-off parts of the realm, to be taught to read and write by the priests, to learn the arts of war in the drill of the Ki-o-to ranks, which were known to be the best in the land. There, too, a young man would learn the fine ways of high life, as a page or a guest of some great lord of the court; for in ways of life, in forms, in speech and in all things else the folks of Ki-o-to set the rule for the rest of Ja-pan, and he who had learnt there could not fail to know. It is said to this day that there are no folks in the world who have more grace in their ways or who are in all things what we call well-bred more than those one finds in the fair Ki-o-to. There dwelt the best learnt folks of the time: men and wo-men who wrote verse and prose; it was a court dame who wrote the first tale or nov-el in Ja-pan. There dwelt the men who first wrote down the past e-vents of the realm, who laid down its laws, and who taught both small and great by what rules they should live to be good. And from the time that they came to know how to read and write, a great deal was made of those things. In most of the fine homes of the great lords there were rooms for the use of an-y one who had the gifts to write, where one could look out on a fine view which should fill the mind with grand thoughts, and write them as they came : the small stand, ink-stone and brush would be sure to be near at hand.

The Jap-a-nese wo-men have done a great deal of such fine work. It was they, not men, as in the rest of the world, who wrote tales and verse, and so gave their speech a form in which it should last. (For a tongue that is used but in speech, you know, will change all the time, and much of the words used by the folks of one time will be lost to their grand-sons.) To write and make-up lines of verse and tales, was one of the ways for the maids and dames at Court to pass the time. It was not a rare thing to find great gifts in these fair ones who were bright and quick of mind, as well as fine to see, with their soft skin and dark eyes, the two black bars on their fore-heads, in the stead of their eyebrows; with their long hair, black teeth, and long, loose robes of rich, bright stuffs. As the court dames of the West, they too could sew and do fine work with silks and threads; could play chess, pet their small dogs, or *chin*, paint shells, as

SILK SHOPS.

well as read a great deal and write some of the best things the Jap-a-nese have in their old books.

Not a few of the fine dames of those days, and sweet young maids, too, chose the life of a nun ; for the Bud-dhist faith soon made the ranks of nuns and monks as large in Ja-pan as the faith of Rome did in Eu-rope. Like those of the West, they gave up the fine things of the world and spent their lives in pray-er and work, and good deeds to the sad and the poor. Some of these great homes took none but folks of wealth and rank, while some bid rich and poor, high and low, come drown their grief in Bud-dha and be as much at peace as they could. Not a few of these were in Ki-o-to, and there a good deal of the fine work was done that still wins so much praise. It was, though, a great deed in these monks to go through the land and raise funds to build a shrine, cast a bell, carve or cast an im-age of some god, or make some such ho-ly thing. The great bells on the monks' shrines of Ki-o-to and oth-er towns, had a fame through the whole land. Some of them were as tall as a man, and cov-ered with rare work, carved or cast. The folks are as proud of this rich work as they are fond of the bells' sweet, soft sounds. It was a great time in the whole town when one was cast. When the chief priest sent forth word that one was to be made, the folks brought to the shrine, coin and gifts of bronze, gold, tin and all the met-als that could be used. These things were put in pots, where they were made to melt with great care, and at last, when the day on which it was to be cast would come, a great fete would be made. The folks, in their most gay dress, would flock to some hill, where, with the priest, they would watch the work-men bring their fires to the right heat and pour their hot flood in-to the mold. Then the crowd, whose joy had grown with each stage of the work, would break out in song and dance and wild shouts, and there would be a grand time for the rest

MEN AND DAMES OF HIGH RANK.

of the day. But Ki-o-to grew and spread more than skill at arms, fine court ways and the Bud-dhist faith through her realm in the Feu-dal Age of Ja-pan. The arts and trades took great strides at this time. Most of us who live in the U-nit-ed States know scarce aught else of what is done in Ja-pan than what we have seen in the fans and a few bits of china, wood and such work.

Now, the men who made things, whose work was a craft, were next in grade to the farm-class, which was next to the Sam-u-rai, who had name and rank. They did not stand high in the scale of caste, it is true, for there was but one class—the folks who bought and sold goods—more low than they. There were a few grades—such as those who play on the stage, who live by alms, tan skins, etc., which the Ja-pan-ese looked on as too low to be named at all. But crafts-men were good, plain folks. They had bright minds for their work, great skill, and much taste, and made work that out-strips all the world in its line. Men who went to Ki-o-to from far-off fiefs would go back to their homes and tell the folks there tales they could scarce think true, of the pot-ter-y and vas-es, the swords they saw, and the fine work in gold and sil-ver and lac-quer and gems that were shown in the shops. No doubt the tales were true, for books we can trust tell us of the same things—some of which are now of the past. Most of these arts and crafts were first taught by the Bud-dhist monks who learnt them in Chi-na. But the Jap-a-nese soon found out ways of their own, and their things soon lost all but a slight trace of the Chi-nese. Some of the best of these crafts-men were still monks — men of Jap-a-nese birth, who spent no end of care and time and work at their bench. They made their things for their shrines, but from them oth-ers learnt to make them for their shops. Some of them would carve a Bud-dha or some god of Ja-pan from a rough log, and put on it months or years of most fine work so as to

OF-FI-CER IN STATE DRESS.

bring out the hairs of the head, the warp of the rich stuff of the robe, and all its fine folds. And such care as one would give to carve his work out of a piece of wood, some one else would spend with his clay molds, or at his sheets of bronze, or the pots of bronze which must reach just the right heat ere it could be cast in a mold. Some made fine in-laid work in met-als, which is a lost art now, and some made lac-quer work. This art did not come from Chi-na, but was found by the Jap-a-nese them-selves some time near 900 A. D. Ech-iz-en is a place that has fame for her great men and scenes of war, as well as for her large stock of fine lac-quer trees and the skill with which her men get and use the milk-white sap, which turns black when it has been in the air for a time, but which can be made red, brown, green, and still more tints. A fine gold lac-quer was made, too, which was of rare worth. To use this paint with skill was an art, to teach which not a few schools were set up in the old days. One made views on land, one on sea; some drew folks, some birds, in-sects, or flow-ers; and some made it their aim to find the best use they could of the gold and sil-ver pow-ders. The art-ists of to-day still turn to those of the Ho-jo times to see the best work that has yet been done in that line.

All sci-ence and art in the realm owe much to the Bud-dhists. They were not all monks who spent their lives in ease. It was by their work that more than one bridge was built, paths and roads were made. It was their thought and toil that set out scores of fruit and shade trees, dug pond and ditch from the far-off streams through fields for rice ; who laid drains where the ground was bad to live on, and who were the first to find more than one new pass through rough hills and up peaks that led to some rare view or made a short cut from place to place. Some of them taught schools, too, or were the wise-heads to whom folks went to learn all sorts of things. They knew the arts to heal scores of ills, and more than one new herb or bulb for the sick or for food has been found by them. Few knew as much as they of the stars and of math-e-mat-ics, to say naught of how well-learnt some of them were in their own faith, and how they would spend years of toil to add one more book to the small store of their shrine or to those of the realm.

CHAPTER X.

THE LONG SWAY OF THE HO-JO CLAN.

It was Yo-ri-to-mo's fath-er-in-law, and not the sons of the Gen clan that took the Great Sho-gun's place. When Yo-ri-to-mo died he left no son so firm and strong that he could take up the work of his great sire and fill the post he had so long held. But there was a man to take his place; one who had no mean rank in the realm him-self. This was the fath-er of Yo-ri-to-mo's wife. He was To-ki-ma-sa, of the good old house of Ho-jo; he was a man of fine gifts, who knew how to use his might, and to get a strong hold on the folks he had to deal with. He soon took his son-in-law's place in all but name, but he did not hold the sho-gun's rank. On Yo-ri-to-mo's death, his son Yo-ri-i-ye, a young man eigh-teen years old, was at once made head chief of all the Jap-a-nese troops, and it was thought that he would ere long take his fath-er's place in all things; but the Jap-a-nese have a phrase which means "There is no seed to a great man;" that is, they have learnt to look for naught in a great man's child. In this case they found their old saw true; for Yo-ri-i-ye had none of the good stuff of his race in him, or, if he had, he let it go to waste while he tried to have a good time. But his grand-sire could wield the rod of the Great Sho-gun, if he could not, and from the time of Yo-ri-to-mo's death, the house of Gen went down, and that of Ho-jo rose. To-ki-ma-sa, and his child, Yo-ri-to-mo's wife, were both folks of more than plain gifts, and they had been of great aid to the Sho-gun from the time he set out to put down the Ta-i-ra; so To-ki-ma-sa knew the ins and outs of his son-in-law's rule as well as most an-y one in the realm. He was made chief of the Coun-cil of State on Yo-ri-to-mo's death, and soon got much of the rights of his grand-son's post in his own hands. He let it seem that he did not know

WO-MAN AND CHILD.

that Yo-ri-i-ye had bad ways, and did not fill his place as he should; but all the time he took good care to put his friends, and the sons of his own house in all the posts in the realm that he could get hold of. So time went on, and when Yo-ri-i-ye was made Grand Sho-gun in his father's place, To-ki-ma-sa still kept the real sway in his hands, and ere long he made Yo-ri-i-ye yield his place to his broth-er, a lad twelve years old, and to shave his head and be a priest in some Buddhist shrine—and there he was put to death by a man in the hire of To-ki-ma-sa. So it came to be with the Sho-guns as it was with the Mi-ka-dos, that he who bore the name was but a tool in the hands of some smart man, full of craft and wit, and force,—one who would stoop to an-y thing to get the rule of the realm in his grasp, and who wove his net so well that both the Mi-ka-do and the Sho-gun were bound in it.

The sway of the house of Ho-jo did not break down as soon as those of Ta-i-ra and Gen had done. It was kept up for near one hun-dred and two-score years, and though none of its sons tried to seize the rank of Sho-gun, twelve of them held all the might of that place. Of these the third, the fourth and the fifth were men of great force, who got a strong hold on the realm, and who did much for the good of the state; some of them made a long search through the whole realm for the best men they could find to put in the posts of trust. One of them was one of the most grand and pure men that we can learn of in the tale of an-y land; he did a vast deal to drive out bad ways and mean tricks, and all such ills as, in all realms, are sure to brew with the men who have a share in the rule. One of the Ho-jo set up at Ka-na-za-wa a fine stock of Chi-nese books, works of the great sage Con-fu-ci-us, of Bud-dhist and of the Jap-a-nese, too; for these folks had learnt monks to write, with all else that the Co-re-ans and Chi-nese had taught them. These books brought scores of men, young and old, to the great town, some to teach and some to learn the laws and the lore of the faith; for there were few in those days but priests who gave their thoughts to books.

In all these years the post of Sho-gun was held for a few years at a time by mere boys, in the hands of the Ho-jo, whose rank had the name of Skik-ken, but whose sway was more than that of the Mi-ka-do. At an-y that they saw fit they would force their Sho-gun to leave his place, that they might put some child, too young to have a will of its own, in his stead.

It was in the Ho-jo rule that Ja-pan had her first great war with folks of a strange land. This was the short fight with the Mon-gol Tar-tars, who, when they had put down the Sung rule in Chi-na and set their yoke on the vast realm of Rus-sia to the West, and held A-si-a in their grasp from the Froz-en O-cean to the Straits of Mal-ac-ca, from Co-re-a to A-si-a Mi-nor, sent word to Ja-pan through Co-re-a, that they would have from the Realm of Isles, gifts and such things as the Em-per-or, Kub-lai Khan, thought meet. Ja-pan must show that she felt him to be her great chief, too. But the Jap-a-nese would do no such thing, and though some men came from Chi-na six times, the Ho-jo sent them back each time with no good news for the Khan. At last the Mon-gol thought he would take by force what he had tried in vain to get by smooth words, and ere long a host of ten thou-sand men were on the shore at Tsush-i-ma and I-ki. All Ki-u-shi-u rose up in arms to meet them. They made a brave set at these strange foes; they slew their chief, and what men they did not kill, they sent back to the Khan with a sad tale of loss to tell him. But he would not give up his plan and at once sent nine men to wait on the head of the realm, to say that they would stay in the Isles till they could bear back some word from the Jap-a-nese throne to their great lord. But they did not go back at all, for all of them lost their heads ere they got to Ka-ma-ku-ra. This of course was a sign for war, and the Jap-a-nese set to work at once to be in trim for the great fight. One more band came from the Khan, and met with the same fate as the last. Then the great Mon-gol set to work to make war on the small chain of isles that would not send gifts to him who had swept A-si-a and felt that he was lord of the whole of the East. The Jap-a-nese had not seen such a sight in all their lives as the great fleet of thir-ty-five hun-dred Chi-nese junks, whose sails made the sea as white as snow, and with-in whose huge hulks there came one hun-dred and sev-en thou-sand men—such an host as Ja-pan had not dreamt of. They came, too, with some of the arts of war that were used in the West—by

COR-MO-RANT FISH-ING.

the great troops of Eu-rope, which were far more sure than the rude ways of the East. What could the small, light boats of the Jap-a-nese do with these great things? Some of them were sunk at once, and though the Jap-a-nese were quick and full of craft so that now they burnt a great ship and now they made their way on board some big, proud junk and cut off the heads of its chief men, the fight for a long time was so close that no one could tell which side would win. Scores of the brave men of the isles were cut down and yet the great foe could not get on land. Each time a force was sent out to the shore it was cut off or sent far out to sea. This sort of strife went on for some time till at last the brave Jap-a-nese cap-tain, Mich-i-a-ri, made a bold stroke that gave the day to his side. He put out from shore with a small band of men in two small boats, and the Chi-nese thought no one would dare to do this in the face of their great fleet if it were not for peace; so they did not shoot at him. But as soon as he was near the great Tar-tar junk he flung out ropes with large hooks on the end of them, that caught a firm hold on the side of the craft and then he and his men leapt on board. Bows and spears were no match for the sharp swords this brave squad now brought forth, and in a short time the close hand-to-hand fight came to an end, and Ja-pan had won. The great junk soon went up in flames and those who had not lost their lives in the fray were borne to the shore in the bonds of their foes. The rest of the fleet, ere long, was made a wreck by one of those fierce storms—which we call ty-phoons—that sweep the west coasts of the Pa-cif-ic in the last part of sum-mer and the first of the fall. It was a scene of woe and of grief and loss that can not be told; and the Jap-a-nese say that it was done by the gods who heard them pray to be rid of their foes. It was the last time that the Mon-gols tried to set their yoke on the Mi-ka-do's realm—and to this day the Jap-a-nese boast that at no time has a strange host left the stains of camp or war on their land. It was the first and last time that an-y realm tried to land its ranks on their shore.

CHAPTER XI.

A BRIEF REIGN FOR THE MI-KA-DO.

In the long list of Mi-ka-dos who sat on the throne while the Ho-jo clan held the reins of state, there was more than one who felt his soul chafe at the bonds laid on him by those who were his slaves by rights; and not a few of them laid plots and made moves, and tried in all the ways they could to thwart their Shik-ken. But it was not till they were off the throne, with heads shaved and priests' robes, that they felt that they could use the strength e-ven of plain men in their realm, which in name held not a man, a child, or an-y thing that had not been theirs while they were on the throne. At last Go-to-ba, who had been a Mi-ka-do till near the year 1200, but was now a priest and a man of much might in the realm, made a bold tri-al to break down the Ho-jo strength; but they beat him in the field and then laid the same hold on the throne as on the Sho-guns. With this they grew still more strong, and so full of pride that their ways were more than the rest of the folks could stand. This led to their fall. There were now no more such great men as had made this race shine in the eyes of all the Jap-a-nese in times past. In these days they had more love of wealth and thought more of ease and their own joys than of the toil and care they should give to their work so as to do their best for the realm. To get means to have all the things they were so fond of, they bore down on the folks for more tax, and at last their proud ways and their three-fold yoke on the Mi-ka-do, the Sho-gun and mass of the folks came to be more than the realm could bear. In the year 1327, or close to that time, the Em-per-or Go-Dai-go made up his mind, with the aid of his son, Mo-ri-yo-shi, to risk life and all

PRAY-ING AT THE TOMBS

else that was dear to him to break down the two-fold form of rule and to get the reins of state once more in the hands of the throne. He knew that the mass of Jap-a-nese folks had so much love and awe for the Mi-ka-do that he would win if he could but get all the troops it would need to cope with the Ho-jo. He got the aid of the Bud-dhist priests, and in a few years made a fort of Ka-sa-gi in Ya-ma-to, while at the same time a brave man, whose name was Ku-sun-o-ki, rose in Ka-wa-chi, who made it the aim of his life to bring back the Mi-ka-do's rule. The scheme of the Em-per-or came to a sad end for him at first. The Ho-jo burnt his fort, got hold of him and sent him to live at O-ki, far off from court and throne. But though they might keep the Mi-ka-do where he could not lead an-y troops on them, they could not clear the realm of its hate for their rule, nor put out the torch which, now that Go-Dai-go had lit it, would burn with a fierce flame till its fire had put an end to the Ho-jo for all time. Twice they laid siege to the strong-hold of Ku-sun-o-ki, but they did not catch him, for he gave them the slip one day and lived to make a grand fight for his lord and a great name for him-self.

For some time the Mi-ka-do and his friends felt that their fate was most dark, but Go-Dai-go kept a stout heart, though far off from his home and in the hands of the Ho-jo guards, and at last there came forth a brave young man to cut the net of the proud Shik-ken and loose the grasp of the Sho-gun rule. This young man was Nit-ta Yosh-i-sa-da. He could trace his line back to the grand old house of

Gen. At the time of Go-Dai-go's war he held a good post in the ranks of the Ho-jo, who sent him to fight Ku-sun-o-ki. But he would not draw sword on the troops of his king, and left the Ho-jo when they bade him do so. The son of the Mi-ka-do, who ruled in the name of his sire while Go-Dai-go was kept from his throne, at once gave him a place in the Mi-ka-do's troops, and then he drew all his own men to him — for in those days each great man had his own band or clan, as in what are known as the Feu-dal Times of Eng-land. So ere long Nit-ta was at the head of a good force and with them led a war on the Ho-jo. It was a hard, fierce strife, but the end of it came when Nit-ta set the proud town of Ka-ma-ku-ra on fire and burnt it to the ground, and so threw down the sway of the great house which had so long held the reins of the realm. At the same time Ki-o-to had been made free by Ku-sun-o-ki and Ash-i-ka-ga, a man whose name came to be great in a few years, and the might of the Mi-ka-do was once more set up in the West. This was not far from the year 1333.

Word was sent at once to Go-Dai-go to call him back to his throne; and now he was not to hold it as a mere tool of some one else, as he had done in time past, but to be in fact as in name the sole head and chief of this land. His first task was to do some-thing for the brave men who had done so much for him. They had won the realm for him, and now it was but fair that he should give them posts and lands such as they would care most to have. The Sho-guns had long made it a rule with the Jap-a-nese that those who fought best for the realm should have the charge of their best fiefs, and with them large clans of men-at-arms. This, then, was to be what Go-Dai-go would do by those who had gone forth to risk all they had for their king. But he was far from wise or just in the way he did this. While he should have made his first gifts to Ku-sun-o-ki and to Nit-ta, he gave three best fiefs to Ash-i-ka-ga Ta-kau-ji, who had fought well, it is true, but not best. He had a great deal of craft and knew how to serve his own ends and to get in the good grace of the Mi-ka-do, so as to raise him-self to a place of much might. He was not like Ku-sun-o-ki and Nit-ta, whose most dear wish had been to break down the might of the Sho-gun and put the full sway in the hands of the Mi-ka-do; but like most of the folks who had fought in their lead, he wished to get rid of the Ho-jo, and when the hard fight of the two most brave men in the realm had torn down their throne, he at once set to work in a still way to put him-self and his house in their place. There was a girl of the Mi-ka-do's house, whom he got to aid him by bribes to make Go-Dai-go give ear to his talk and his plans, while with the folks he made the most for his own ends out of some small ill-will that was felt by those who had held low posts in the ranks and had fought well to put down the Ho-jo, but felt ill-used now at the scant way in which the Mi-ka-do had paid out his spoils. These men were more fond of war than of peace. They did not care if there were two heads to the realm or one, so long as the Sho-guns were not in the hands of the proud race of old To-ki-ma-sa. Thus Ash-i-ka-ga soon found that he could shape things to suit him-self, and that in a short time he could start up more war and strike for his own high prize. It was a blow to him when Go-Dai-go made his own son Sho-gun, which was still a post of great pride in the realm; but he did not show his wrath and laid plans to get his own way in the end. The Mi-ka-do had been a man of grand force and will when he first held the throne, but he had lost his best gifts while he was in the bonds of the Ho-jo, far off from his throne and all that was dear to him. No one had known him to be so weak and vain in the old days, but now the words of Ash-i-ka-ga and the young girl whom he had paid bribes to talk for him had so sweet a sound in his ear that he did not stop to think if they were true or false. He let them get a strong hold on him and would not heed the wise men round him who bade him take care and think of the rest, who had done as much or more than Ash-i-ka-ga to serve him. His thoughts all went to this one man. He did not treat Nit-ta as he should have done, and he did not place Ku-sun-o-ki in such a post as he had the gifts to fill. No doubt this man could have done more for the good of Japan just then than an-y one in the realm, to say naught of what was due him for the great work he had done in the field of war.

The prince had not been Sho-gun for long when Ash-i-ka-ga made the Mi-ka-do think that his son had laid plots to get the throne; and when the Prince, stung to the quick by his hate for this base foe, and wroth at the lie he had told his sire, gave the word to his troops to march to Ash-i-ka-ga and pay him up for his tales, Ash-i-ka-ga made it out that the Prince's plan was to snare him first of all, so that he could be more sure of his way to the throne. In this way he got the Mi-ka-do in so great a rage with his son that he gave word to have him dealt with as if he had in truth turned foe to his sire.

But the doom of bonds and death had scarce been laid on his good son when the Mi-ka-do saw he had been made a dupe of, and, though it was too late to bring back his boy, he at once grew cold to his real foe. Ash-i-ka-ga saw the change, fled from Ki-o-to with great bands of the men-at-arms who did not like the ways of things at court, and took

I-DOLS.

the place that the Ho-jo had held at Ka-ma-ku-ra, which he had built up since the fire. Then the Mi-ka-do went back to his first friends. Nit-ta was freed from a charge that had been laid on him that he was false to the throne, and was put at the head of the Mi-ka-do's troops to whip the bold Ash-i-ka-ga. But the odds were not on the Mi-ka-do's side this time; he had lost the love of the ranks once glad to die for him, and so his force was small, while that of his foe was large. His side lost in the fight that came on, and he had to flee for his life with a small band of his men who still held true.

Ash-i-ka-ga was lord of the field, but he had fought the throne, had drawn arms on the Son of Heav-en, and so to the Jap-a-nese he was worse than an-y of the Ho-jo. Then he tried to make his wrong deeds seem right and give to the realm a new Mi-ka-do. He sought out Ko-gen, a child of one of the em-per-ors who had been on the throne ere the time of Go-Dai-go. Some of the folks thought he had no right there now since the real Mi-ka-do's son Mo-ri-yo-shi was in all ways fit for his sire's place. But Ko-gen took the seat, and this new Son of Heav-en soon made Ash-i-ka-ga Great Sho-gun, with all the old state of that post at Ka-ma-ku-ra. So the two-fold form of rule was set up once more, in less than three years from the time it was thrown down. But the change, and still more the fact that Ko-gen had been put on the throne, brought on a war in which Ash-i-ka-ga and the North, fought the South and the real Mi-ka-do. It was kept up for near three-score years, and is known as the War of the Chrys-an-the-mums.

This is a long tale of false deeds and true blue, of fire and fight, of want on the part of the poor folks, and waste on the part of the rich; and though at first it was a sharp strife to put down the claims of one Mi-ka-do and fix his foe firm and sure on the throne, the true aim was lost at last, and the whole realm was a scene of strife, and the war was but the brawls of small chiefs for the sake of land—or for no good cause at all. Ere it came to an end all the great chiefs who had led in it were dead; the Mi-ka-dos them-selves came to feel that it was of small note to them how it came out, for most of the men-at-arms seem to have lost sight of the fact that they had come out to give the throne to their true Mi-ka-do. At last, in 1392, Ash-i-ka-ga sent a band of his men to the Em-per-or of the South, who held old Go-Dai-go's place, to ask him to give the sword, the glass, and the ball (which he had borne with him when he fled from Ash-i-ka-ga's men) to his Mi-ka-do, who held his court in the North. He, they said, should be Em-per-or, and the Mi-ka-do of the South should be ex-em-per-or, and from then on the throne should be held by a son of first one house and then the oth-er. The things were sent, and the change made with great pomp; but the Jap-a-nese say to this day that the line of the South was that of the true Sons of Heav-en, while the line of the North was false—and that, ere long, died out. All Jap-a-nese books that are thought to be worth an-y thing by the folks, speak of the Mi-ka-dos of Ko-gen's line as the "False" em-per-ors or North-ern em-per-ors, which means the same thing.

CHAPTER XII.

NIT-TA AND KU-SUN-O-KI.

In all the long fight of the war of the Chrys-an-the-mums, there were two men whose brave deeds make them stand out from all the rest who took part in the strife. These were Nit-ta Yosh-i-sa-da and Ku-sun-o-ki Ma-sas-hi-ge. They now fought for their king as if he had used them as his most dear friends while he had his sway, as if they did not know how he had let the base Ash-i-ka-ga take what was their due, and had lent his ear to that man's tales of Nit-ta's bad faith. None of this did they let stand in their minds when once more the Mi-ka-do had need of their strong arms and their great minds on the field of war. Once Nit-ta sent word to Ash-i-ka-ga, "Come out and meet me and fight with me. It is we who lead the two great bands ; come forth and we will fight hand to hand ; the side of him who lives shall win the war, and so we may spare the blood-shed of our men." The Sho-gun's men got him to say that he would not do this, but ere long they found a chance to cut down the brave chief of their foes with-out an-y risk to their own. He had set out with some two or three score of men to arm a fort one day, but he had not gone far when near three thou-sand of the foes fell on them in a small path through some rice fields near Fu-ku-i. He had no shield, and their darts fell round him like rain. His men said fly, but he would not leave them, and put the whip to his horse to get near to his foes, so as to fight them with the sword, but one arrow struck the poor beast while he was at full speed, and its mate gave a death blow to the chief as soon as he rose. It struck him full in the forehead and gave him scant time to draw his sword and cut off his head, so that his foes could not tell his corpse from those of the rest of his band. And the rest went, too, by the hands of the false ranks or their own: for it was more grand and good in a Jap-a-nese of those days to die with his chief than to live on when he was gone.

Nit-ta's corpse was found, and his head was set

up at Ki-o-to for all to see; but his grave was made near the spot where he fell, and to this day it is a spot that the Jap-a-nese love, and they keep fresh flow-ers on it all the time.

Ku-sun-o-ki died not in the field, but by his own hand. His plans were set at naught and he lost his fights in the field, so that he felt that there was but one thing for him to do; he must die and leave his name pure. This seems strange to us, but to the Jap-a-nese, five hun-dred years a-go, it was the part of a great man.

It was said that of all the men in Jap-a-nese his-to-ry, Ku-sun-o-ki stands first, for the pure love he bore his land, for his strong brave heart to risk his life for her sake, and for the way he would give up an-y wish of his own to serve his king. The boys learn his life, and think of him as their best type of a true Jap-a-nese knight, and look on him as the great-est man their land has had—as we look on George Wash-ing-ton. They could tell you how he was taught in the lore of Chi-na by the priests; how strong he was of limb, too (for when he was sev-en years old he could throw a lad twice his age in a wrest-ling match). While he was taught in books, he was taught in the arts of war as well; and was so apt in this last that he cut off the head of a foe when he was but twelve years old; he was taught the forms of drill that the Chi-nese used when he was fif-teen, and made a vow to him-self that the aim in life should be to throw down the rule at Ka-ma-ku-ra and give to the Mi-ka-do his rights—this sway that had so long been kept out of the hands of the

JA-PAN-ESE BOATS.

throne. So he took up arms for Go-Dai-go, and though the Ho-jo tried hard to get hold of him, his side won at last, with the aid of Nit-ta and Ash-i-ka-ga. Then came those years when he was so ill-used, and Ash-i-ka-ga took the place he ought to have had, but which could not turn his heart from his king an-y more than it did Nit-ta's. Thrice they drove the troops of the false Ash-i-ka-ga out of Ki-o-to, and when he fled to the West it was Ku-sun-o-ki who said, "Go on, catch him, and break up this strife he is at the head of." But the Mi-ka-do did not see fit to make use of his plans, and so it went on, as we know, from bad to worse, till, in spite of all these two great chiefs and their brave bands could do, their cause was lost.

When Ku-sun-o-ki made up his mind to die, he said good-by to his wife and his babes, and went to a farm house near the small town of Sa-ku-rai, where he gave the sword (which was a gift from the Mi-ka-do) to his son and bade him think of his sire, a-venge his death, and bear arms as a good brave man should. With that he took his life, and near a score of his band—men of his own race—died with him.

CHAPTER XV.

I-YE-YAS-U AND THE HOUSE OF TO-KU-JA-WA.

WHEN the Tai-ko died he left his heir, his cares, and all the plans that were so dear to him, in the hands of I-ye-yas-u, whom he had learnt to trust long ere he rose to his high post, and whom he had made next to him-self in the State and the Dai-mi-o of eight fiefs. His son had been wed to the child of I-ye-yas-u, who made an oath that he would fill the Tai-ko's place till the boy came to the age when he could rule.

I-ye-yas-u was a man of great parts and of much fame, and he made laws with most, if not quite as much skill as he made wars, which is a great deal to say. His first deeds of note were done while he was in a low place in No-bun-a-ga's troops, from which he rose till he was one of that great chief's first men. He fought well, too, in charge of part of Hi-de-yosh-i's ranks; and in times of peace he built him-self a great cas-tle. On the fall of the Ho-jo he took the small fort near Yed-do bay yu-ki, was a great man both at books and in arms. None of the men who had charge of the Sho-gun's work in the Ash-i-ka-ga Age were so great as he, who tried to raise the folks from some of their poor ways and took more than one step to drive out some of the great wrongs in the forms of rule. He held his post in the name of the Ash-i-ka-ga heir, Yosh-i-mit-su, whom he was to teach and take care of till he should reach the age when he might rule. He did not do as old To-ki-ma-sa did with the son of Yo-ri-to-mo, but gave much thought to have the youth learn a great deal from the best men in the realm, from books, and in all the arts of war. He saw that his friends were well-taught young men of first rank, with gifts and skill for all that a young Jap-a-nese lord of those days should know. This lad was the grand-son of the sire of the house, and was the one man of his race who bore the name of the "Great Ash-i-ka-ga." He was made Sho-gun and put at the head of the troops when he was but ten years old, and ere long he won great fame by his brave acts in the wars of the South and West. But through one rash act, the cause of which must have been his great love for war, be brought the curse of his land on his race as well as on his own head. This act was that he sent a band of Jap-a-nese to Chi-na near the year 1400 with gifts and fine words, by which they made it known to the proud Em-per-or of that vast realm that Yosh-i-mit-su felt that this great Mon-gol had a sort of right to be the chief of Ja-pan as well as the rest of the East, but that he would beg him to own that Yosh-i-mit-su was Nip-pon— or King of Ja-pan. It seems to have been done for naught else than to get for the Sho-gun the grand name of king. He did not dare to try to get the Mi-ka-do's throne, though he had long dwelt in as much style as his lord. There was no real cause why the realm should have been made to thus bow her head to Chi-na, and the man who did it brought hate on his name for all time. If the whole land had not been in a bad state he could not have done this base thing, and as long as his house held the reins of the realm, in name or in fact, things went from bad to worse.

In these days there was a great deal of change at the head of the state. Some-times the rule was at Ki-o-to, where both the Mi-ka-do sat with the court that ruled him, and the Great Sho-gun with his Shik-ken, more than one of whom in this age held the reins from both the Sho-gun and the Em-per-or. Some-times the seat of rule would shift to Ka-ma-ku-ra, where a plain sho-gun had sway, or was the tool of a man whose rank was not as great as his own, though he had more strength of will.

Much of the time the heads of the two towns were in feuds, as were the clans of most all the realm, so that not much else took place in the land but fights for clan-pride, for rights to lands, and no end of such things. Each clan chief dwelt in a great house that was like a fort, and in whose walls dwelt scores of his men with their wives and small folks. The homes of the monks of Bud-dha, too, were like the store-rooms of a great guard-house. More than once it was by their aid that a side won. To be in trim for war was the plan of all who could bear arms. This strife went on for years and years: towns were burnt, fields laid waste, all were made poor and the folks of high birth as well as the low fled to the hills, where they might dwell in caves to be out of the sound of strife: and young folks grew up with no one to teach them. By-and-by dearth came, as it does in all lands in the wake of war, and thousands of folks, young and old, died for the want of food. Men who had been born to live on farms were made to join the ranks at arms, while some of them grew to be thieves and spent their time in raids on towns or on the roads, where they would rob an-y one they could catch. And the Mi-ka-do was as bad off as his folks. He had no wealth. He dwelt at Ki-o-to, which was at all times in the hands of a force-at-arms—if not those of the Great

Sho-gun, then it was those of Ka-ma-ku-ra, the troops of the East.

To this day, if the Jap-a-nese want to tell a tale of great woe and wrongs, or if they want to make a play of folks who did no end of bad things, they

A BRONZE WARE-HOUSE AT YED-DO.

say it all came to pass in the time of the Ash-i-ka-ga.

It was near the close of this age, in the year 1542, that a great man by the name of No-bun-a-ga came on the scene to throw down the sway of the proud house that had brought so much ill-luck to the realm, to break up the bad ways of the Bud-dhist priests, give a good word to a new faith, and bring back in part at least the old and long-lost might of the Mi-ka-do.

He came from a race of Shin-to priests, but far back he could trace his blood to the great Ki-o Mo-ri and the house of Ta-i-ra. His sire had borne arms, and, as most of the men of an-y note in those days, his aim in life was to get hold of all the lands he could win. When he died, he left his arms, his land and his feuds to his tall, brave son, who bore his charge well. Six fiefs or states did he add to those of his sire and much wealth did he gain, so that in a few years, he rose to much note in the realm. In Ki-o-to he built him a fine house—a cas-tle. He was so great that he had the man of his choice made Sho-gun in spite of all those who did not want him could do. In one of the old books of Ja-pan it is told that this prince was a man of large frame, but of fine, pale skin, which the Jap-a-nese do not think well of in a man. But the book says that he had a heart and soul that made up for all else he might lack; he was brave and bold, and held high thoughts on what was right and wrong, and would see that folks had their just dues in all things where he had a voice — and it was not long ere he had a voice in all things. His wit was keen, his will strong, and it was a rare thing for him to be wrong in his plans, though his foes did call him "Lord Fool" at first. He had been taught in all the arts of war, and of all men of his time he was known to be the best to take charge of a set of troops, to mark out a camp, lay a siege, or hold out when one was made on him. He made use of no head but his own. Now and then he would ask for the views of those who were with him, but it was more to find out their hearts than to have the aid of their brains.

He read the hearts and the minds of all the men he met, but he let no man read him, and when he made up his mind to do a thing he gave the word and it was done. He had no small ways and held no mean thoughts for an-y one; he was just and some-times more than just, and gave good words and good gifts with a free hand. But one thing did he hate. That was a false heart. An-y one who did not hold true to the land of his birth, to his em-per-or or his creed of right and wrong, was so low and base in the eyes of this great prince that he lost no chance to show him up in his true light.

It was this hate of what is false, that led him to make a great war on the Bud-dhist priests;

and it was his love of what is just and fair that made him hate the Ash-i-ka-ga and spend his all to give the Mi-ka-do his rights in the rule of his folks. Though at first he was on good terms with Sho-gun rule, he got in a feud with the man he put in that post at Ki-o-to, and when he had held sway for six years or so, No-bun-a-ga drove him off, and broke up the might of the Ash-i-ka-ga house, though it had held the realm in its grasp for near a hun-dred and fif-ty years. Then for two-score years Ja-pan had no Sho-gun, for this great son of Ki-o Mo-ri's line, though the chief man of the realm, could not trace his birth to the Gen race, and no one else could be the Great Sho-gun. But he had charge of the troops, and held the post in all but name.

With the aid of his right-hand men—four great gen-er-als whose names rose to fame in more ways than one—he brought large tracts of the realm, which still held off from the Mi-ka-do's rule, to own his sway. Like Yo-ri-to-mo he had great skill and force of will on the field; but he could not bring the chief clans to bow to him nor could he hold in peace those whom he had won in war as Yo-ri-to-mo did. Still he was a great man, and his name will live with the Jap-a-nese through all time.

But he has more fame as a man who could rule like a king, who could set up and pull down Sho-guns, and drive out a race which had held sway for hun-dreds of years, than as a great chief in the clan-fights. He did one more work, more great than all these and a work for which the Bud-dhists in Ja-pan still look on him as their worst foe, as one for whom they can not feel too much hate,—though their faith ought to teach them not to hate at all.

No-bun-a-ga saw that the whole band of the Bud-dhist priests of that day was full of wrong and guilt and that most if not all of the priests were false to their creeds and their vows; and he took it on him-self to break down the worst sects and purge them of their pride and vice, while at the same time he took pains to treat well the priests of the faith of Christ who came from the West in the same year that the name of No-bun-a-ga was first heard through the realm. He had been brought up with priests when a child, so he did not feel for them the awe that most folks had. He had been taught in the Shin-to and did not like the Bud-dhists an-y way, and so was more quick to see their sins than he would have been if he had been taught to feel that they could do no wrong. He saw that they were not a great cult of pure, good men whose one thought was for their faith; but that they were like the rest of men—and worse, some-times. They had rooms full of arms which they could use as well as the Sho-gun's troops, and with which they oft left desk and shrine to fight in the clan wars. But in those times of such great strife, they might have done this and done well if their thoughts had been for their books and their faith when they were at home; but in place of that they made their faith a cloak for an-y thing they might want to do — and they grew to want to do all that an-y men did, and a great deal that some men would not do. Their chief place was on Lake Bi-wa, and there this sort of life was at its worst, and when the priests were not at grand rites or in their rooms at feasts and wines and all sorts of "good times," they were deep in schemes to make them-selves more great in the eyes of the folks and to foil the plans of No-bun-a-ga. In turn for this, he made up his mind to wipe them out. Of course he did not make an-y talk of this till he felt that the time had come to act. Then with his vast ranks he camped near the shore of the Lake and told his chiefs to set fire to the great town-like cas-tle of the monks. The chiefs heard this with awe. Since the year 800 this grand old place had stood, and it was thought to be the home of some of the best men in the world; it was the strong-hold of the whole realm a-gainst the Prince of Wrong. At first they did not think their chief could mean what he said, but he told them of how he had rid the realm of thieves; had run an-y risk to his life for the sake of his lord on the throne at Ki-o-to, that he might at last bring peace to the land; he told them that he had learnt that there was no worse ill in the land than this great seat of the Bud-dhists, which for the same cause that he had fought the rest of his fights, he now bade them send up in flames. Then he told them what he knew of the aims and the lives of the priests. So, at his word, his men went on to burn shrines and homes, and to ply sword, lance and dart to all who dwelt with-in those walls. Old men and babes, dames, maids and priests all met with the same fate. At last it was done. The

AC-RO-BATS.

great Mon-as-ter-y of Hi-ye-zan was no more. No-bun-a-ga's first blow at Bud-dhism fell with a force that crushed all in its way. This made the rest of the priests dread and hate him more than they had in times past. But for all that he kept his place at the head of the realm and grew more great and strong all the while. Nine years from the time the Mon-as-ter-y on Lake Bi-wa was burnt, two of the Bud-dhist sects whose views were not just the same, got in a sort of feud, and made so much talk that the Mi-ka-do was told of it, and word was sent out that No-bun-a-ga should hear the rest of their talk and should be their judge. This was done and an end was put to the feud and to one of the sects, whose views it was thought would do harm to the State.

For twelve years one of the chief seats of No-bun-a-ga's Bud-dhist foes was the great Mon-as-ter-y of O-za-ka. Their feud with him was that he let the Cath-o-lics come in from the West and build up their shrines and spread their faith. These Bud-dhists made their home a place where the foes of the great chief could hide from him, and there plots to thwart him were laid. No-bun-a-ga knew all this, but he was a man who could bide his time with his foes — and at last his time came. One day, when his troops were out near this great fort of the monks, some of his best men were slain by a band of what the Jap-a-nese call "grass-reb-els" (that is, men who watch for and shoot at their foes while they hide them-selves by some bush or tree). As soon as they had shot their darts they fled to the fort of the monks. At this he set out with a will to serve this strong-hold of the Bud-dhists as he had done that on Lake Bi-wa. He laid siege to it; some tried to fly and were slain; post on post had to give up to the troops of the great chief; and scores of men, wom-en and babes were put to death. At last the Mi-ka-do, in grief that so much blood was shed, sent three of his men from Court and a Bud-dhist priest of a sect at Ki-o-to, to beg them to yield, which they did. No-bun-a-ga's foes gave up their fort, with all their shrines, their homes, and the things that were dear to them, in-to his hands. From then till now it has been held by the State. The chief said he would spare those who still lived; the priests were to live with oth-er monks of their sect, but their might and pride was gone; and at no time since has the faith been so strong as it was ere this great siege. More than once since then the Mi-ka-dos have had to take steps to check them when they bore too high a hand; but it was not a hard task, for the faith nev-er got o-ver the blows dealt to it by No-bun-a-ga.

Now the prince, in his zeal to rid Ja-pan of these old sects that had grown to be a curse to her, gave the aid of his good will to some priests of the Church of Christ, who came from far-off Por-tu-gal, to bring, as they said, a new faith to the Jap-a-nese, but who, in truth, did naught but bring them a new bane.

They had come in the wake of some sea-men of Por-tu-gal, who had a taste that led them to cruise in strange seas, and were cast by storms on the shores of some of the south isles of Ja-pan. This was in the first days of No-bun-a-ga's fame, and near the same time that the folks of Spain got their foot-hold in our own land, which, like Ja-pan, was then new to all Eu-rope. The Dai-mi-o on whose coast these men were cast, sent word for them to go and see him (which they did) and he used them well. He gave them the means to go to Go-a, which was the chief town of the Por-tu-guese states in In-di-a, and he got them to say that each year they would send him a ship full of such goods as would sell in his towns. This they did, and once, when one of these ships lay in port, An-ji-ro, a Jap-a-nese of Sat-su-ma, who had slain a man, fled to it to hide, and was borne off to Go-a. There he met the great saint of the Church of Rome, Fran-cis Xav-i-er, whom the king of Por-tu-gal had sent to his lands in In-di-a to spread the faith there. From him An-ji-ro heard of Christ. Ere long he took the new faith in place of his own, and came to be so well-learnt in all that was taught in it, that the great priest would have him help to spread it in his own land. So, with a few more men, they went to Ja-pan and set to work in Sat-su-ma in 1549,—the year in which No-bun-a-ga fell heir to the lands of his sire. From there they went on and though in some fiefs they met with kind words and crowds to give ear while An-ji-ro told them what the great priest said, and in some they found most of the folks cold to them; still they kept on, and not a few of those who heard them were baptized. At last Xav-i-er lost heart. When in Ki-o-to he found that war and trade were the two great thoughts of the folks, and that he could find no chance to see the Mi-ka-do or the Great Sho-gun. He made up his mind to give up his work there, but he left the seeds of the new faith in more than one soul, who took up the task of the Saint. In five years from the time Xav-i-er left Ki-o-to, there were six of their church-es in or near Ki-o-to it-self, and scores of them had sprung up in the South-west. At the time of No-bun-a-ga's death more than a hun-dred thou-sand Jap-a-nese, of all castes, had come to be Cath-o-lics, and there were two hun-dred of their church-es in the realm. The Por-tu-guese brought some-thing more than a new faith to the Realm of Isles. It was they (and on their first trip, too), who brought the first guns and pow-der that the Jap-a-nese had seen, and taught them how to make the fire-arms which in a few years were used a great deal through the whole realm. To this day there are not a few folks in the realm who think that Christi-an-i-ty and guns mean much the same thing; and link with both the thoughts of a world of grief and ills that they brought.

CHAPTER XIV.

HI-DE-YOSH-I, OR THE AGE OF THE TAI-KO.

No-bun-a-ga had four chiefs who were most as great as him-self, and who, with him, rank as some of the best men-at-arms Ja-pan has had. The first of these was Hi-de-yosh-i. The folks of his day gave him the nick-name of "Cot-ton," for he could do so ma-ny things, and cot-ton, you know, can be used in a long list of ways. Then there was Go-ro-za, to whom the folks gave the name of "Rice," for the great chief of the realm could no more do with-out this bold man than they could live with-out rice. Shi-ba-ta was known as "At-tack," since he had great pluck and skill to drive down hard on the foe. And as I-ke-da could draw his force off the field so well that they scarce knew when he was on the weak side of a fight, he had the name of " Re-treat."

In time there came to be a fifth chief in No-bun-a-ga's ranks, who was more great than all but the first. He was I-ye-yas-u, and that name, with those of No-bun-a-ga and Hi-de-yosh-i, we are told, stand first in all the list of Ja-pan's great men.

Hi-de-yosh-i, the first to take the place of his great chief in the realm, was born of farm-folk, but he did not go out at morn with grass-hook in hand and bas-ket on back to cut grass for the live-stock all day, nor did he hoe the weeds in the wet rice-fields; but he made the streets his school, his work-shop, and his play-ground. His wits were keen. He was quick and had no fear of an-y thing or an-y one, and there he learnt the ways of men and grew sharp and shrewd. While yet quite a small lad, he went to be a groom to the brave young chief, No-bun-a-ga, who knew the men that took care of his steeds as well as those who rode as his staff. He thought he saw signs of great gifts in this small, mon-key-like face, and bright eyes that could not keep still. So one day he told him that he ought to bear arms and learn to fight, and some day he might lead in great wars. So the small street boy went in-to the ranks of the realm, and rose from post to post till he was a gen-er-al. He was still young, but he bore him-self so well that when he was thir-ty years old he was made a prem-ier or chief of first rank. Of course there were not a few in the troops and in the State who soon made them-selves his foes; for in a land like Ja-pan, where rank is of such great note, few like to see a man sprung from plain farm-folk reach such a height as this. But Hi-de-yosh-i's foes could not do much to hurt him. To show their spleen they said he was a "Crowned Mon-key," but he bore the crown of his might and fame with worth and pride. His rise was a strange thing to more than his foes, for none but lords of the Fu-ji-wa-ra blood took this high place; but he got the right to it some way through brave deeds and work, craft and wit, push and will; and the Em-per-or gave him the right to found a house of his own, which is known as the Toy-o-to-mi. As was the way with Jap-a-nese, he had had three or four names in the course of his life ere this; but now he took that of Toy-o-to-mi Hi-de-yosh-i, by which he is best known in his-to-ry. We are told that he was a man of war from his youth up. His troops were fond of him, for he bore him-self like a true knight. Where was seen his flag there men were sure was the thick of the fray, and the worst of it for his foes. This flag had one gourd on it at first, but as a new one was put for each fight won by the knight, it soon had a large bunch of them.

A WED-DING.

On the death of his chief, No-bun-a-ga, Hi-de-yosh-i went at once to the town where the man who had put No-bun-a-ga to death had set him-self up in his lord's place, and slew him. He was now more great than an-y man in Ja-pan. A hard fight was made for one of No-bun-a-ga's sons to keep him out of the first place in the realm. But it was in vain, in the end; and at last this "mon-key face" boy from the farms of O-wa-ri went back to Ki-o-to the head man of the realm.

For years he gave him-self up to toil of all kinds for the good of the land,—and much he did for it, too, both in a way to make the soil bring forth more than it had done in times past, and to put more sway in the hands of the Em-per-or.

To keep his men-at-arms at work in times of peace, he built most grand pal-a-ces at Ki-o-to, and did a great deal in more ways than one to make that fine old town more grand than it had been ere he came. He paved the bed of the stream Ka-mo with broad, flat stones, and tried to make the place great as a port as well as in all ways else. Nor did he do these things in no place but Ki-o-to. His gifts for the arts of peace were more great than for war, and the whole realm was made to feel them. He chose the site of the old monks' fort at O-za-ka for a fine new town, which he laid out on a large scale, built walls round it, and made a vast fort there and a pal-ace where the Mi-ka-do and not a few great men dwelt in af-ter years. Then he had the bed of the stream which flows by it made more broad and more deep, and dug scores of can-als, and made the way clear for the town to be a great place for trade in years to come. You may some-times hear folks call this town the Ven-ice of Ja-pan.

In those days the post of Na-ga-sa-ki was a place of much note in trade, and for that cause Hi-de-yosh-i took it from the Dai-mi-o and put it in the hands of the crown. His whole life now was spent to serve his great lord. For this cause he spared him-self no toil to make the folks do their best in all things they put their hands to. At no time, ere then or since, has Ja-pan made such boats as were then built; at no time has she had such large trade in so ma-ny things as she then had. Her men went far and wide on the high seas, as you could not think they had ev-er done if you knew them now. Their ships were twice or thrice the size and of much more fine build than the junks that now hug their shores or ply their way to Chi-na or Co-re-a. The ships of the great Co-lum-bus were not so large; and they could sail as well and as fast as the craft of the Dutch and the Por-tu-guese, which won world-wide fame in that same age. The Jap-a-nese knew how to sail them, too; and went in them to the lands of the South and South-west, to the Ma-lay Ar-chi-pel-a-go and the Ku-ril-es on the North. In more than one of these lands you can still find folks whose sires were Jap-a-nese sea-men. It was in the time of peace, more than in his wars, that Hi-de-yosh-i's best gifts came out. When he had once won his high place in the realm, all his work and thoughts were for the best good of the State and its true head. For this he would not rest in times of peace, as most men-at-arms, but toiled as hard to build up towns, to push on trade, to make new plans by which to bring a more large and sure tax in to the Em-per-or. While he thus held the reins of the realm with so strong a grasp, he made the folks, both high and low, like him and look up to him; for he was a man whose aim was to be fair and just to all, and in this rank, name, race or deeds done to him-self, did not move him. He was frank and free to be friends with those who had fought him, and did not put his foes to death when he had won in a fray with them, as had been the way of No-bun-a-ga. The brave chief I-ye-yas-u at first bore him ill-will for the high rank he had got; for he felt that he should have had the great No-bun-a-ga's place; but Hi-de-yosh-i got him to come to Ki-o-to at last to pay his court to the Mi-ka-do, and ere long he had made him his friend once more; and I-ye-yas-u took Hi-de-yosh-i's sister for his wife.

In the year 1591 he gave up his high post of Ku-am-ba-ku to put his son in his place, and from that time on he was known as "The Tai-ko." His son was but a child, and he made this change to make sure that the rule of the realm should be kept in his own race; but as long as he lived he kept his grasp on the realm just the same, and the whole time from No-bun-a-ga's death to his own, is known as the "Age of the Tai-ko"—the pride of Jap-a-nese his-to-ry. Like his old chief, Hi-de-yosh-i felt that the strength of the Bud-dhists was a source of dread to the state, so he went on in the work of No-bun-a-ga to take it from them. He broke up the great Mon-as-ter-y of Ku-ma-no, whose priests laid claim to a large fief which brought them much wealth. But the Tai-ko was no friend to the new faith brought from the West by Xav-i-er and the priests of Rome. He saw that these deep men, and some of the Jap-a-nese whom they won to their creed, took care to gain the good-will of the great folks of the realm as much as to spread their faith. He saw, too, that where they had a hold in a town, or an-y part of a fief, there might be seen a change in the way the folks felt as to the rule of the realm; and in more than one case, he saw signs of priest-craft that bode no good to the State of Ja-pan. He found that the priests won their way a great deal by much show and a free use of gold, which the kings of Spain and Por-tu-gal gave them for "alms." He saw that some of them took pains, by false means and fair, to make the folks look down on the Bud-dhists so that they would be the more quick to take the new faith. He found that the priests were all ruled by their Pope, a sort of church king, whose word was law, and who was held up as a man who must be right in all things. He wore a trip-le crown, the Tai-ko learnt, and in the name of his God, set up or threw down thrones, took the crown from the head of one prince to put it on some one's else, cut the realms of Eu-rope in parts to give them to his friends, and as far off as in the New World seemed to have the might to give lands to whom he chose.

"This man's priests," said Hi-de-yosh-i to him-self, "may want to give him Ja-pan to deal with in the same way. They have sects of some size now on our coast, and they have a church in our chief town." No-bun-a-ga had been their friend, but he felt sure that they were not the friends of the Jap-a-nese State, and ere long he found that he was in the midst of a dark plot they had laid round his son—the heir to the Ku-am-ba-ku—in his own house. He told this to his friend and chief-at-arms, I-ye-yas-u, in whom he had put more than one great trust ere this. I-ye-yas-u set to work at once to find out if there were grounds for his lord's fears. He found that three of the Dai-mi-os—each of whom was lord of a large fief—had sent word to the Pope that they threw them-selves at his feet, and felt that he must be their great lord, as he was the one man in the world who stood for the God of Earth.

The Tai-ko did not need to know more than this

TEA AF-TER THE BATH.

to prove that there was good cause for his worst fears, and he made up his mind at once to cut all the strings that ran from Ja-pan to this far-off Pope for good and all. But he took time to act, so that he could make his stroke tell all the more when it fell.

He took near a year to lay his plans for the great blow he thought to strike. At length in June, 1587, his troops were at their posts in the fiefs of Ki-u-shi-u, and the South coasts of the realm (in the lands of the false prin-ces), and there were such hosts of them that they could quell an-y who might try to beat them back. At last the day came for him to give the sign, and from end to end the realm rang with the word of the great Tai-ko, that in the name of the Mi-ka-do, Chris-ti-an-i-ty must be put down in six months, its priests from strange lands must leave Ja-pan at once and for all time, on pain of death; its schools must be shut; its church-es torn down; no cross or way-side shrine should be left to stand in an-y part of the realm; and all Jap-a-nese who bore the faith of Christ must give it up. The men of the West of course, had to leave, and at first the Jap-a-nese priests fell back, and the Church of Rome seemed to have had a great check in the land; but the work went on in a still way just the same, and thou-sands of Jap-a-nese took the name of Christ each year. Ere long the priests threw off this cloak and came forth once more in their robes, and taught in the streets as they had done at first. Then the Tai-ko bade them leave, and not a few Chris-tians were put to death; but it was left till the time of the next rul-er to drive them quite out of the realm.

Hi-de-yosh-i gave up his war on the Chris-tians for the sake of a long-dreamt-of plan to bring the lands to the West of Ja-pan in-to the Mi-ka-do's em-pire. Once, when he had some words with the Chi-nese Em-per-or, he made the boast that he was the King of Nip-pon and king of him-self and he should know how if he chose to do so, to make the Em-per-or of Chi-na bow to his yoke. Five years went by ere he set out to make his threat good. Then he sent a call to his lords and their clans to take up arms and form ranks for a vast host that he would send to the coast of Co-re-a, which, though then at peace with Ja-pan, did not pay her court to the Son of Heav-en as she should. It had been his chief aim from the time he was a boy, to make Co-re-a—if not Chi-na, too—a part of the Jap-a-nese Em-pire. He had tried to get No-bun-a-ga to let him do this when he was a young man, and though his chief had heard the plan with a laugh, Hi-de-yosh-i still kept his mind on it. In their last weak years the Ash-i-ka-ga had let Co-re-a cease to send her gifts and pay her court to the Mi-ka-do, as she was bound to do by the terms Yo-i-to-mo made with her king; and the sea-thieves that were so thick on the coasts would scarce let an-y trade be kept up. This was a state of things that the Tai-ko could not brook in the land he thought should be to the Mi-ka-do like a part of Ja-pan. Ere he made up his mind for the war, he sent two bands of men to Co-re-a to ask in the Mi-ka-do's name the gifts due him. The first band did not get there, but the next one did. Then, the Tai-ko heard from some Chi-nese who came to dwell in Ja-pan, that their own realm was in a state of much strife and bad home-war, and he sent word to the Em-per-or of the Ce-lest-ial Em-pire (as the Chi-nese call their realm), to say that if he would not give ear to Hi-de-yosh-i's plan to have Chi-na pay court to the Mi-ka-do, that the Jap-a-nese hosts would march on him.

What at last brought the great chief to the point of war, shows how grand was the stuff he was made of. He lost a child for whom he had great love, and his grief was deep and strong. Though, as as was the way in those times, he had eight or ten wives, he had few chil-dren, and when this one died he could do naught but mourn for months. One day he went off to a shrine, where he sat for a long time, lost in his sad thoughts, while his eyes were bent on the sky of the West, in front of which rose the far-off hills. All at once he cried out, "A great man ought to use his troops in the lands of the West, and not give way to grief;" and with that he went back to his home, sent a call to his chiefs, told them that they must aid him to make Chi-na bow to the Mi-ka-do's throne, and at the same time win lands and wealth and fame for them-selves. They all fell in with his plan and ere long a fleet of junks set sail for the land of Co-re-a, which they were to take first. Hi-de-yosh-i had laid out all his plans, and told his chiefs and his rank and file just what to do. It was a grief to him and to them that he was now too old to lead them him-self. They had had signs from the gods that bade them be of good cheer and they should win their cause in the great, strange lands of the West. They made a clean sweep in the first part of their march through the land, and the king had to flee and leave his town in their hands. When calls were sent to Chi-na for help, a great tide soon set in that drove them back at once; but the Tai-ko had thought of this and had a large fresh force made up to send on in case of need, and as soon as the news got to him, the new ranks went out and the plan to push on in-to China was to be put through with great force, when the Tai-ko fell sick and died. So, a truce was made. More lives than we could count were lost in Co-re-a for no just cause, and so great a drain had been put on Ja-pan that not a few of the poor folks at home lost heart for work, and sold them-selves to the men who came from Spain and Por-tu-gal, for slaves.

So this last act of the great Hi-de-yosh-i's life was a blot on his name. It was the cause of no end of grief and pain and loss to the folks for the good of whose realm he had done so much to gain. But the Jap-a-nese do not blame him much for this. Not a few of them feel yet that Co-re-a is theirs by right and that it was meet she should have been shown her place and the might of her Em-per-or, the Mi-ka-do.

Both of these great schemes, like his acts to the Chris-tians, seem to have been laid out by long years of thought, and with the view that they should help him to gain the great aim of his life, which was to crush the strength of the clan-chiefs and put the realm in the sole sway of the Mi-ka-do—a state of things which Ja-pan has but just got to in our own age. But he did a great deal to bind the fiefs to the throne, and his last wish was that the clans would drop their feuds, blend their aims and give their strength to the best good of the realm as a whole.

The Jap-a-nese have much cause to think well of the low-born Hi-de-yosh-i; and it is with pride that the men of to-day look back on the things that he did which made the "Age of the Tai-ko," like that of E-liz-a-beth of En-gland, the best their realm has known.

CHAPTER XVI.

THE LONG PEACE.

From the time of I-ye-yas-u, Ja-pan kept her doors closed to all the world for two cent-u-ries and a half, till the tact of our own Com-mo-dore Per-ry broke the seal in 1853, and got her to make terms of trade and good-will with the U-nit-ed States.

A few Dutch-men were let to stay on the small isle of De-si-ma, and to have a ship go to them once a year from the Dutch East In-dies; but no one could come on it to stay, nor could an-y one leave by it; and the isle was quite shut off from the main land, with which the Dutch could have naught to do. No oth-er ships could touch at a Jap-a-nese port for an-y cause; and it was a hard task for a Jap-a-nese sea-man cast on the shore of a strange land to get back to his home.

In the mean-time the Sho-gun, in his fort-like cas-tle at Yed-do, with its vast guards, was the real head of the Em-pire, while the Mi-ka-do had no guard to awe the realm, but dwelt in his plain home, to found a great town—a site which Hi-de-yosh-i had shown him as the best place for the seat of the Ku-an-to. In the few odd times that he was not in the field—for war is the one word that tells what those days were—he was at work in his town, in the time of both his chiefs. He took but small part, if an-y, in the plan to put the yoke of Ja-pan on the Em-per-or of Chi-na; and he was at Yed-do when he heard that the Tai-ko was sick, and went to him at once. He was by his bed when he died, and swore to take care of his son and to do all he could to have him take the place of his sire. But few folks thought that this child was the Tai-ko's son, and, more than that, there were not a few who felt that Hi-de-yosh-i had had no right to rule them ("The up-start," they said, "who was naught but a low-born clod and a groom"). They had borne his sway, since they could not help it, but they were up in arms at the plan that his son—if he were his son—should take his place. Not a few thought that I-ye-yas-u had his own eyes on the post; and then when the hosts came back from Co-re-a, it was not strange that a home war should have come up, since some of the chiefs had not been on good terms while off in the West, and not a few had cast their own eyes in the way of the Tai-ko's place. War did not break out all at once, but the feuds and the small fights, and the want of trust in I-ye-yas-u grew till at last it was a plain fact that his foes were at work to land a large force and put him down; while he, for his own part, had his troops, and his friends had theirs in fine trim to meet them an-y time they chose to come out. They came ere long, and in the great fight on the plains of Se-ki-ga-ha-ra, not far from Lake Bi-wa, the Gen prince won the day. So great a fight and one so sure in its ends Ja-pan has not seen ere that or since.

A GOV-ERN-OR.

It was long and hard, but I-ye-yas-u and his men

would take no rest when it was done till they had got hold of all the chief points in the realm and the whole of Ja-pan was in their hands. The two cent-u-ries of war and strife in the realm were now at an end, and a new age of peace was come which was to last for two hun-dred and fif-ty years.

Now, both of the chiefs whom I-ye-yas-u had served had been men who could not trace their blood to the Gen race, and so they could not hold the post of Great Sho-gun; but he was sprung from that grand old stock; the blood of the Mi-ka-dos, of Nit-ta, and more than one of the chiefs who had brought East Ja-pan to bow to the throne was in his veins, and he had the force and the chance to make his name out-shine all his sires. The Em-per-or, sick at heart of the strife that had held sway in his realm so long, now had one great wish—that was, peace. In I-ye-yas-u he saw one who had won such a high place in the minds of all the Jap-a-nese by the way he had fought on the field of Se-ki-ga-ha-ra, by the fine state in which he could make up and keep his troops, and by his skill found and build a great town, that he felt him to be the one man in the realm who could bring back peace, hold the feuds in check and start the folks to work and trade once more. So the realm had a new Great Sho-gun and the house of To-ku-ga-wa be-gan a rule of more than two hun-dred and fif-ty years; for the race of I-ye-yas-u held its post till a few years a-go, when the great change of 1868 came to the realm, and an end was put to the Sho-gun rule for the rest of time.

When I-ye-yas-u found him-self the lord of most all Ja-pan (though in name, you know, he was a sub-ject of the Mi-ka-do; and in rank, though not in strength, the Ku-ge, or lords of the court, were born more high than he), his first thought was to fix things with the chiefs and the clans who held lands and had large bands of men in their train, so that there would be peace on all sides—a peace that should be sound and sure, and have its root in his own hold on them. It took great skill and much thought to do this, for the whole realm, as we know, was cut up in fiefs, which were in the hands of Dai-mi-os, each of whom had the sway of a king in his own lands, and by tax drew from them large funds. For the most part each fief had been held by the same race of folks for a long time; and so each chief was the head of a large house, with a great deal of pride and rights and small feuds and all such things which are most hard to smooth down. Then, too, the Sho-gun was a man who was one of them-selves till he won the chief post in the realm by his might at arms. Now he would put on airs and turn them out, too; for he had a large house of his own to look out for and must make more than one change in these fiefs so as to get each of his own sons in a place of wealth and note and might, in case an-y one should try to raise a force to break down his sway. But I-ye-yas-u had a great deal of tact and, ere long, he had set all this right, and was on good terms with the Dai-mi-os, too. He first made it known that he would grant to all who had been his foes in the past, terms of good-will if they would have them. That is what we call an am-nes-ty. He sent forth word that he would like the past to be put out of mind, for it was a grief to him that so much blood had been shed; and now he would like to see all the clans in the realm on the best of terms. By such words as these and by more than one good turn to his late foes, it soon came round that most of the clans were soon on good terms with him. He did not try to force those that still held off; for he thought they would do like the rest in time if he let them be; but he took good care to fix them so that they could do him no harm; no two clans of foes were left side by side; and in more ways than one he cut off all chance for them to join in a large band to bring more strife with him.

Then to cut off one more great source of war in the past: he made up a guard for Ki-o-to, so that no one could seize the Mi-ka-do. With both of these things done he felt sure of his hold on the realm, and could turn his thoughts to works that should make that hold so strong that it would last for cent-u-ries. One of the first of these to claim his time was the new town of Yed-do, to which he brought a vast host of work-men to make the cas-tle more large, to dig moats and can-als, to grade streets, fill in the marsh lands, and to build. Fleets of junks brought stone from Hi-o-go for the walls of the fort, and for the gate-ways of the town. These he set up, far out-side of what most folks thought would be the bounds of the town; but I-ye-yas-u fore-saw how it would grow. He had a great moat dug that went round both fort and town, and left much room to spare; and great gate tow-ers were set up, though no wall was as yet built to make them of an-y use; and the folks had to take such a long walk out in the fields to see them, that they would laugh at them. The Sho-gun said the time would come when walls would be built, and that they would be too small for the town. His word came true, and in two-score years the lands on the East side of the stream were built up.

And the great I-ye-yas-u had plans and works to be done for more than this fair town of his. He built up new and made sound the old forts of the

Ku-an-to land till it had from ten to a score of fine, stout cas-tles. He seemed to know what would be the growth and the needs of the Em-pire in the years to come, and not a few of his plans were the means that brought that growth. One thing he did was to build fine roads through the realm, one of the best of which is the To-kai-do, a broad way that still skirts the East-ern Sea and runs from Ki-o-to to Yed-do, or To-ki-o, as they now call it. He set up near three-score posts on these roads, each with a good house, where folks could stay at night, where they could change or hire steeds to take their goods, or slaves—known as cool-ies—to bear their packs or the "pal-an-quins"—which are small cars that all folks of note in Ja-pan used to ride in from place to place. The old roads, too, had a great deal done to them; and there was scarce a pass through the hills, a bridge, or a foot-path of much use, that he did not have put in good shape, while all the points where folks had to cross streams by boat—and this has to be done a great deal in Ja-pan—he made to have a broad place to land the boats at both ends of the routes. Now all this was a vast deal of work, and it was work of great note, and good, too; for in those days the lords of the court and the chiefs of the fiefs, with great bands of their men, had to go from place to place a great deal since they were made by law to dwell in some of the chief towns for a part of each year. The Sho-gun had quite a long code of rules laid down, which these men had to go by when they took these trips; for Ja-pan is a great land for rules and laws on how the folks shall act at all times—what we call et-i-quette. I-ye-yas-u made ma-ny laws, from those on

NIGHT PO-LICE.

small things that have no place but in the house, to the large ones of the clans; and they were laws that spread till they went in-to force through the whole realm.

But twice were there breaks in the sweet peace of this great Sho-gun's rule. When the Tai-ko died the

Chris-tians had thought they would be free from the ban that had been put on them, since they had a good friend in his son; but the fight at Se-ki-ga-ha-ra put quite a new face on things, for I-ye-yas-u had seen too deep in their ways in Hi-de-yosh-i's time to want them to go on with their work in Ja-pan, and now the Dai-mi-os of the fiefs gave them some of the same sort of terms they, in times past, had thought meet to use on the Bud-dhists they had forced to take the faith of Christ. The Jap-a-nese Chris-tians were told to give up their new creeds, but they would not; and at last they took up arms in their cause. Such a thing as the farm folks armed to fight their own cause was so new in Ja-pan that I-ye-yas-u felt sure that the priests were at the root of it. He would not have been quite so sure if he had not known that the priests paid their court to the Tai-ko's son as if he held the place his sire had left him. The Sho-gun's next step was to send forth word that all Chris-tians should give up their faith; but the priests and folks soon went on in the old way, and kept up their work to bring more to join the church all the time. This was the way it had been in Hi-de-yosh-i's day, but I-ye-yas-u had set out to make the work sure this time. But he was not in too great haste. On the watch for all the craft and plans of the priests, his men one day found a chest in a deep well, and in it a vast hoard of gold, with a roll that gave sure proof of a plot he had long known some-thing of. He found in this that plans had been laid to make the prince of one of the fiefs king of Ja-pan, and to yoke the realm to one of the em-pires of Eu-rope. On this, the Sho-gun lost no time to make clean work of his task. He sent all folks not born in Ja-pan from its shores at once, and said that all Jap-a-nese must give up the faith of Christ or leave the land. This was in the year 1611, and in a few years more he had a short strife with the son of the Tai-ko, and then Ja-pan was free from war for a long time. Hi-de-yosh-i's son, though put down in fair fight, still had some thoughts for the place of his sire, and with some Jes-u-it priests, and others, who did not like the Great Sho-gun, was at the head of a band bound to do him ill. I-ye-yas-u found this out, and in a short time he made some cause to march on the youth, who was at the cas-tle of O-za-ka, which was set on fire. Then a fierce fight took place, in which I-ye-yas-u won, and the son of the Tai-ko lost. Then, for years and years, the faith of Christ was shut out of the realm, and so were all folks of strange lands but a few Dutch on the isle of De-si-ma. This was the end of blood-shed for more than two hun-dred and fif-ty-three years. How sweet that long peace was to the poor realm that had had to bear so much woe and grief and loss for such a long time!

I-ye-yas-u was not like most men who win in all the wars they fight. Peace was more dear to him than strife; and the last years of his life were spent in the fair cas-tle that he built when he was a young man, on the first lands that had been giv-en to him. There he gave his time and thoughts to the good of the realm—how he could best wipe out the deep scars of war that lay on her; how he could best bring forth in her the arts of peace, and fix his plan of rule so that it should stand for a long, long time. When he died he bade his sons rule in ways that are both kind and just. The great tales that are told of the pomp and state with which this man was laid in his tomb, and all the rites that were held at his death, show us a good deal of the ways of the folks at that time, and how much they thought of the grand rites due the dead.

I-ye-yas-u's son took his place, and seems to have kept up the work of his sire in all his plans. He did what the great To-ku-ga-wa would have done if he had lived; and in his time, the strength of the Yed-do rule grew more sure with all the clans, the forms of rule of the realm were made better, and the fair town of Yed-do grew in size and strength and fine looks all the time; but it was the

Iyeyasu and the House of Tokugawa.

grand-son of I-ye-yas-u who next to him ranks as the best man of all the new line of Great Sho-guns.

JAP-A-NESE AR-MOR.

He it was who brought the Sho-gun rule and clan-strength to their height. He made the Sho-gun more than the chief of the Dai-mi-os, which was his real place; he made the post in its way most as great as that of the Mi-ka-do, and ere long the Dai-mi-os came to be bound to pay court to him and to do his will as much as if he were their Em-per-or. He, too, did much for Yed-do, and laid new plans

JAP-A-NESE AR-MOR.

for her, such as wa-ter-works, look-outs for fire with bells to tell by a code of signs where the flames had been seen and how far they had got. The gold that had been found in the Isle of Sa-do in I-de-yas-u's time, was now made in-to coin at the mints set up by his grand-son. A law was made to fix weights and meas-ures. For the first time, the realm was gone o-ver and maps made of the fiefs and the strong-holds of the Dai-mi-os. The great shrines which I-ye-yas-u had set out to build, he went on with ; and in scores of ways did he start new works and plan new ways that have been of vast worth to the realm in times past, and are kept up to this day.

This Sho-gun was the first to use the name of Ty-coon. It means some-thing like, " I am a great man and you must think much of what I say." The Sho-gun had no right to it, but his pride was strong, and one time when he had some Co-re-ans come to him, he felt that he must make them feel that he was of great note in the land. To the Jap-a-nese it did not mean much, though some of them came to use it them-selves in the time of the last three Sho-guns, when they had a wish to treat their lords with great awe. But when the first of them used it him-self to our Com-mo-dore Per-ry, it made a great time ; it was a large part of the cause of the war that soon came on and broke down the sway of the Dai-mi-o chief and led to the new state of things we now find in the realm.

CHAPTER XIII.

THE ASH-I-KA-GA AGE.

The race of the Ash-i-ka-ga, whose plots so soon broke up the Mi-ka-do's sway, kept hold of the reins of the realm for two hun-dred and fif-ty years. Thir-teen of its sons were Sho-guns, and in all their time you can find but one bright page in the long, sad tale of their age, when ill-will was in the air and there were fights for small clan feuds all the time, and now and then for great ones, when the whole land would be drawn in-to war.

In the time of the Ho-jo it had been the right of the Court to say who should hold the post of Sho-gun, and then you know it was the Shik-ken who had the Sho-gun in their hands, so that they had no might of their own; but when the Ash-i-ka-ga then got the post for their own race and had it go from sire to son, the man with the rank was not at all times the man who had the sway. Much of the real work of the state was done by smart men, not of high rank. One of these, Ho-so-ka-wa Yo-ri-in the midst of a park with a fence round it, at the far-off Ki-o-to, where lords of the court, priests, men of rank and blood, of books and art, let the days slip by in home-work and ease. The folks used to say, " The Sho-gun all men fear ; the Mi-ka-do all men love."

The Em-per-or him-self was in awe of the To-ku-ga-wa Sho-gun. He gave full sway to Bud-dhism, for that did not teach folks to think ; but it was a crime to take up an-y of the thoughts or plans of Eu-rope or the New World. No one could so much as build a boat on the plan of those used in the West; or on an-y plan but that of a Jap-a-nese junk. To go out of the realm to see what was done in the rest of the world, to learn an-y tongue but those of Chi-na and Ja-pan, to have an-y of the ways of the Eu-ro-pe-ans, or to hold to the faith of Christ, were crimes that naught but death could pay for. When the Sho-gun and his train went out, the folks had to bow their heads to the earth. He was the real head of the Em-pire. Each fief of note was like a small realm, whose dai-mi-o was a king with hun-dreds of men in his train, but the Sho-gun was their king. Such plans as they laid to watch all that was done in the realm and keep the folks un-der their thumbs have scarce been known an-y where else. The realm was full of spies ; no one had trust in an-y one else, and so all the folks, high and low, came to be far more quick to lie than to tell the truth. Most of the dai-mi-os who had got their lands from the Sho-guns felt that their court was due to him as to a king, and

STREET MU-SI-CIAN.

the folks of the low castes, for the most part, did not know that the Mi-ka-do had ev-er had an-y real sway in the realm; they thought him sent from Heav-en to be their great high priest, and while they felt all awe for him, they did not feel that they ought to serve him as they did the Sho-gun. Most of them thought the "great and good house of To-ku-ga-wa" had had sole right to rule from the first. The Sho-guns knew they had no real claims to all this, but they were bound to keep their place; and so, lest the folks should come to know the truth, they made it a great point to keep them in the dark. They must not be taught to read or to think much for fear they should find out the past his-to-ry of the land; and as much as could be, the high castes, too, were kept from such books. This may have been one cause why such a fierce fight was made on the Chris-tians and on all folks of strange lands; they were bound to teach the mass of the folks.

Thus shut in, years went by. They were years of peace and of good crops, and not of want. The farms brought forth all the food the folks could eat; there was no trade with the rest of the world; no one could mass great wealth; there were no out-side folks to spread new thoughts and plans, and a calm lay on the land that was sweet, as peace must be when a realm has been long at war. But it was a kind of peace that was not for the real good of the realm. The Sam-u-rai, who had the sole right to wear the sword, were the on-ly ones who could take up more than the most plain stud-ies; and no two of

meet and talk long but that a spy was by
hat they said. Now, you know, the Jap-
:ome to be fond of books ; not a few of
ai were men who had read and thought
l ; and no Sho-guns could blind their
truth, nor keep them from the work in
took so much joy. Some of them saw
plans of the To-ku-ga-wa, and chose to
eat task which would show them up at
spite of all their pains would tell the
th as to their realm. This great task,
)me of the chief Sam-u-rai gave their
, write the first His-to-ry of Ja-pan. The
)ok the lead in this was the Prince of
lived till the year 1700. He drew round
of men who had read and thought a
and with their aid made his great work,
ar the size of our own Mr. Ban-croft's
the U-nit-ed States, but makes two hun-
or-ty-three of their books. The men
pure Chi-nese, which is still thought to
t tongue in which to write a work of
just as in times past Eng - lish folks
t-in the tongue in which they ought to
st works.
Prince of Mi-to had great fame for his
wrote a good deal ; and as he had some

ties of blood with the house of To-ku-ga-wa, he was more free to state his views than an-y one else in the realm. But his views were not for the good of the Sho-guns; he thought they were wrong to do as they did, and in his book he led folks to see that the Mi-ka-do and no one else had a right to be head of the realm, and the Sho-guns from the first had been mere thieves who took the might from the throne. From the first Mi-to's work was made much of by well-learned men, but for more than a hun-dred years there were but a few cop-ies of it, and all of them were made by hand. Its views spread more and more, though; and less than two-score years a-go there was such a great want for it that it was put in print. But ere this came to pass, some one else took up the same line of work, and told the his-to-ry of all the great clans. This too laid bare the facts of the rise of the Great Sho-guns, and brought forth the rights of the throne. It told its tales in such plain terms that some of the books had to be gone through and purged more than once ere the sage and well-read men at Yed-do (who had to judge and pass all works ere they could go out in print) would let it be put forth.

Now, with these two great works on the past in their hands, and with the time to think that the long peace gave them, it is not strange that the Jap-a-

A JAP-A-NESE WRI-TER.

nese grew to feel that their realm was in quite the wrong hands. Nor was this the sole wave that had set in to hold up the Mi-ka-do's rights to his folks. The priests, too, found more time for thought now, and not a few set to work to bring back the old Shin-to creeds as they had been held ere the Bud-dhist faith came to change their tone; for Bud-dhism made a vast change in the Shin-to. This, of course, brought folks to think more of the ho-ly line of the Em-per-or, of the high rights of the throne, of what some of the Mi-ka-dos had done of old, and of the great men who had fought for them, and spent life, wealth and all in their cause. With this not a few of the well-learned men made up their minds to go back to the stud-y of the old Jap-a-nese books, and to make more of their own tongue, which for a long time had been quite put down by the use of the Chi-nese in books, in state pa-pers at court, and with all the folks of high rank. Now the Sho-guns tried to check this, but the Mi-da-do, the court lords at Ki-o-to, and some of the chief Sam-u-rai did all they could to help it on. They wrote a good deal, and in not a few of the chief fiefs of the realm their works drew the folks of mind and might to see the Mi-ka-do and the Sho-gun in a new light, and to think of plans to put down the rule of Yed-do and set up that of Ki-o-to. This rise of the

Shin-to schol-ars and the works that they wrote, with those of the Prince of Mi-to and his friends, led to a great change in the views of the Jap-a-nese, which at last threw down the whole scheme of Jap-a-nese Feu-dal-ism. In the course of years, with the calm that seemed to lie like a pall on their life, they grew to feel that they had gone back in their growth, while the rest of the world went on. The sea, which had once been like a wall to shut them in, had come to be the road that led strange ships to their shores; for not a few ship-wrecked Jap-a-nese got back to their homes on board A-mer-i-can boats, scores of which went by in sight of her coasts each year. The Rus-sians came down from the north and set up their claims to part of one of the north isles, and Eng-land, France, Hol-land and A-mer-i-ca all had a wish to trade with her. All these signs told the wise that some day ere long there would be a stir in Ja-pan, which if it came would end in the fall of the Sho-gun. Now there were a few who felt that a war might be made on them some day by the "wild men" of the West and the New World. (Most of the Jap-a-nese thought all A-mer-i-cans and Eu-ro-pe-ans were a half-brute race, or "wild men," as they said; for they had been the curse of Ja-pan in the past; they had taught them of pow-der and fire-arms, and had been the cause of a great deal of woe and blood-shed.) No plans were made at Yed-do to meet these "wild men" if they should come, but not a few of the great dai-mi-os of the South thought it best not to wait for the Sho-gun's lead, and set to work to have their vast clans in trim in case of need. They had two needs in mind; one was to meet the "wild men" that they did not fear to speak of; but one that they had kept to them-selves was that the time might come ere long when the Mi-ka-do's own cause would want their arms. And if it were the home foes or the "brutes," one or both, they had made up their minds that their troops should be a match for an-y they might meet. These were men whose sires had been bred to arms for a-ges, and they were not so bound up in Ja-pan that they had not seen that the arts of war in the West were far a-head of their own; and so, while the realm lay in a calm of peace the great chiefs of the South got the men who had learnt Dutch, and French, and Por-tu-guese, to put the books on the arts of war (which they had got hold of in some way) in-to the Chi-nese or Jap-a-nese tongue, so that they could learn from them how to dress and drill and fit out their troops as was done in the West.

One of the chief of these dai-mi-os was the Prince of Mi-to—for that great house had in 1840 a prince who could well bear the name of him who wrote the

His-to-ry of Ja-pan a hun-dred and fif-ty years be-fore. But he who took the real lead in plans to teach the Jap-a-nese the arts of the West was the Prince of Sat-su-ma. He was a man of brains, will and wealth. As a wise prince as well as a great and good one, whose peer could scarce be found in the realm,

THE WAY THAT PLAIN FOLKS TRAV-EL.

it was his aim to spread the stud-y of his-to-ry, as well as all the best Jap-a-nese works of an-y kind, through the realm. He spent time, wealth and thought on his fief to make it bring forth all it could, and got his troops in-to the best shape then known to Jap-a-nese men-at-arms; for he saw that the time would soon come to march on Yed-do. And he saw, too, more than most of the chiefs what would be the needs of the realm when that had been done, and so he did what he could to get young men to learn the Dutch and Eng-lish speech, and to find out through them what the rest of the world knew of the arts of war as well as of peace. He was king in his own fief, and did as he chose there, and of course no one thought to check his plans. He set up some mills and shops where great guns were cast as the Dutch made them. He saw that the young men of Ja-pan ought to go out and see the rest of the world and learn how things were done there; and by and by a score of the most bright youths of the land got off in one ship to Eu-rope, in spite of the Sho-gun's care and watch. Then some more slipped off to Eng-land and the U-nit-ed States. This prince was well known through all the realm, and young men went to him from all parts of the land, to be with him in his schools or to learn the arts or plain work-a-day trades which were not seen else-where in Ja-pan. His chief town was full of life, and in it were some of the most bright and well-learned folks and most skilled work-men in the whole realm. By this time it was plain to a large part of the Jap-a-nese that the time of the Yed-do rule was short, and the Prince of Sat-su-ma was to be the man to lead the out-break; but in 1858 he died, and his great work fell to the hands of those he had trained and taught—nor were they weak when their time came.

All these great chiefs of the South were of stock as old and as good as that of I-ye-ya-su, and though he had made his way to the head of the realm and the rest had had to bow to him, they did not love him nor his house an-y the more; and it was gall to their sons to be the slaves of his race. Some-times one or two of them would not do the Sho-gun's will, but step by step, from the first stage when they were his "friends," and went to Yed-do as his "guests," till now when they were as his slaves whom he bade come and pay court to him, the To-ku-ga-wa had borne down on the Dai-mi-os a bit more hard each time till now there was but one way to free the realm from their grasp, and that was to break out on them in a vast host, raze Yed-do to the ground, tear down the Sho-gun's throne, and drive the race

A MAN OF THE CIT-Y IN WIN-TER DRESS.

of I-ye-ya-su forth to find lodge where they might —or death if they should face round.

This they had grown to feel that they would do if the worst came to pass. But for a long time they kept it all in their own breasts, like a fire in a mound, while in a still way things went on in-side to make the heat more fierce, and e-vents took shape with the Sho-gun and the rest of the realm that were to wake the flame at last to do the most that a-ny of them dreamt of.

CHAPTER XVII.

THE LAST WAR AND THE DAWN OF A NEW AGE.

Most folks think that our Com-mo-dore Per-ry was the sole cause of the late war in Ja-pan; but that was not the case. We know that the clans had long been in wait for a chance to break out on the Sho-gun, and they found it when he let him-self pass for the Em-per-or with Com-mo-dore Per-ry. To be sure it was our brave sea-man who got the realm to un-lock her ports to the world, and the long peace came to an end in a great fight on the folks who went there from A-mer-i-ca and the West; but not

Last War and the Dawn of a New Age.

Sam-u-rai and the dai-mi-os who led in
re glad to have the "wild men" come,
ey fought for was to break down the Sho-
d set up that of the Mi-ka-do. It was
one else who brought on this last dread
ealm of isles. But the A-mer-i-cans lit
ınd this is how they did it and how the

m-mer of 1853 the still air of Yed-do Bay
ly day to shrill sound that came from the
leet of A-mer-i-can steam-ships. Their
not go round to the port of Na-ga-sa-ki,
y the isle of the Dutch, when he was
he in terms that no one could call rude,
ıld stay where he was. He sent some
Em-per-or of Ja-pan, with let-ters in
ked in the name of the Pres-i-dent that
or would be friends with the U-nit-ed
come to some terms of trade with her.
did not get to the Em-per-or at all, but
ʼun, who took them and read them and
as to act on them all by him-self, for he
n in the place of the Em-per-or, and
not go well for me if these new folks
not he." So, when he had made up his
:o say to our brave Com-mo-dore, he sent
ıch note who taught in one of the great

schools of Yed-do to treat with him; and this man, to give his lord a big name in the eyes of the strange folks, let his men speak of him as the "Tai-kun," a Chi-nese word which means "great prince" or "high lord," and if used at all was not due an-y one but the Mi-ka-do. But it was a term that meant no real rank to the Jap-a-nese, and so the Sho-gun told them, but to Per-ry he let it stand for the same as Em-per-or. Now our Com-mo-dore knew that there was a Mi-ka-do at the head of the realm, but he thought him a sort of pope, or chief priest, while the "Ty-coon" was the Em-per-or of the state. So when he came back home he felt that he had made the right terms, and that all had been well done to make Ja-pan and A-mer-i-ca good friends. But this was far from the case; for while the Sho-gun held the reins of rule there was no name but the Mi-ka-do's that stood for the Jap-a-nese Em-pire. It was not at all the voice of the realm that said yes to the great change. They are not head-long folks, and it was a vast thing to them to break the seal that had so long shut out the rest of the world for the fact that those whom they had once let in had done them harm and had laid plots to make them slaves to some strange king whom they had not seen and scarce heard of. And more than that, the Mi-ka-do and his court were full of wrath at the lie the Sho-gun had told when he let him-self pass for the Em-per-or. The To-ku-ga-wa gave a great poke them-selves to stir up the fires that lay in the depths of the great clans of the South ; but still they were kept hid and peace lay on the realm for some years. The realms of Eu-rope sent their ships in the wake of Per-ry's *Sus-que-han-na,* and it was not long ere some of the best ports of Ja-pan were bound to let the "beasts" and "wild men" of the world come and go as they might choose. But, in 1859, when the ships came and a real flood of trade set in, the realm woke from its long sleep with such a shock as it had not known in all its life. In the first place the folks had not thought that all these ships would want to bear off so much goods as they did to their own ports. So when they had bought up their loads there was not much left and the cost of plain things rose so high that the poor could not have them, and that brought want and woe at once. At the same time the land was swept by earth-quakes, storms, floods, and fires, all of which the mass of folks felt to be due in some way to the "wild men" whom the Sho-gun had let come to their ports. In the midst of all this woe and want and fright the Sho-gun died, and left the choice of a new one to his Re-gent. Now of the two young men of the To-ku-ga-wa whom the lords thought of to take the post, the Re-gent chose the one whom some of the chief dai-mi-os did not want ; and when they made some fuss a-bout it he put them in jail ; and with them not a few of the best Sam-u-rai in the realm—men of state, chiefs at arms, and some who were most sage and well-learned —were put in bonds, sent to far-off parts of the realm, or had their heads cut off. The Re-gent was in great straits, for he knew that the terms with the out-side world could not hold good with-out the Mi-ka-do's own name to them ; and while the "brutes" made loud calls to have their treat-ies made good, the Mi-ka-do and Court would have naught to do with them. At last, in fear that the " wild men" might force their way in and make no end of bad work, he set his own seal to the terms he had made and sent word to Ki-o-to that he had done so. At this the wrath of the Court broke forth and a cry of hail to the Mi-ka-do and out with the "wild men" went from end to end of the realm. The Re-gent had been false to his chief, it was felt ; and all through the land thou-sands left their homes and said they would not go back to them till the Mi-ka-do, with the rule in his own hands, should drive out the strange folks who had come in on them. Then there was a time of strife and blood-shed, when the land swarmed with bands of low-caste men, armed and in for fight, with no heed for the laws of the land or of man to man. The Re-gent was slain, and so were scores of folks from the out-side world. The Sho-gun's sway was on the wane; few of the clans held to the Sho-gun, while the eyes of most of the realm were bent on the throne, and the will of the Mi-ka-do was that for which the folks gave ear. The dai-mi-os of the South came out strong and left Yed-do to make Ki-o-to their seat, as it was that of the Court. They put funds in the chest of the throne; their troops—the best in the realm—were at the Mi-ka-do's call. All at once the Yed-do chiefs said they would close the ports and get the folks of the West to leave Ja-pan; and they sent some men to Eu-rope to see to this; but in the mean-time, at the wish of the Ku-ge, the Mi-ka-do sent forth word that all who were not Jap-a-nese should leave the realm. Then arms were raised on their ships by the Cho-shi-u clan; the Sho-gun sent word that they should not be fired on, but they were. The Sho-gun's

LA-DY IN THE RAIN.

might was gone; the Mi-ka-do was come. This was in Ju-ly, and through the rest of that sum-mer the two sides stood in arms face to face, and with each the ill-will and dread of some-thing worse to come grew and grew. In the fall new ills came. The Sho-gun side said that the Cho-shi-u, with some of the Ku-ge, had laid a plot to get hold of the Mi-ka-do and set up their own rule be-hind the throne, as had been done in the past. This drew on them the wrath of all the Yed-do clans, and put them in a bad light, for they could not get clear of such a grave charge at once, since they had tried to have the Mi-ka-do leave Ki-o-to and take the lead of their troops. The clans thus paired, the realm was in a bad state for some time, and in mid-sum-mer of 1864 at the gates of Ki-o-to they came to a fight which was kept up for two days with great strife and loss of life. It was lost to the Cho-shi-u and gave the Sho-gun's band one more taste of their strength, though that strength would have been much less if it had been used to hold up their own throne in place of the Mi-ka-do's.

In the same month a fleet which bore the flags of four na-tions of the out-side world sent out its fire and shell on the fort of the Cho-shi-u till it beat them down and paid them off for their fire of the same month in the year past. But their ranks were fine and well-drilled, their hearts were true, and

THE FIN-ISH-ING TOUCH.

they were not to fail in the end. It was an all summer's fight with them and the Sho-gun side, which came to an end with loss and rout and shame to the To-ku-ga-wa, and the last fall of their sway. The poor young Sho-gun whom the Re-gent had set up, worn out with his cares, died in the fall, and left one thing done—he had got the Mi-ka-do to say he would make terms with Eu-rope and A-mer-i-ca— but they must be his own terms, not the Sho-gun's.

The young man who next took this post was the one whom the Ku-ge had made choice of in the first place; and when he had been in it some eight months one of the chiefs most true to the Mi-ka-do, got him to give it up. This was one great step in the way of the full sway of the Mi-ka-do. But there was much still to be done; for the gates of the Pal-ace were in the guard of a clan that was the most staunch and true of all that still held to the To-ku-ga-wa; and as they had the Mi-kado they were yet at the head of the realm. The chiefs of the great clans of the South would not rest till the work that had gone so far should be well done, and they made up their minds to work as one band and by a bold stroke to wipe out the post of Sho-gun and the might of Yed-do, and to give full sway to the throne on which now sat the young Em-per-or Mut-su-hi-to. It was on the third of Jan-u-a-ry,

1868, that they did it. The troops of these chiefs by a quick move took up their posts at the gates of the Pal-ace, sent out the Ku-ge who were in wait on the boy Em-per-or and would let no one go through the gates but those who held the same views as their chiefs. The Court was swept clean of all who would set up aught but the Mi-ka-do's rule; and from the throne there went forth the good news that the Em-per-or and his Court would now have sole rule of the realm, and that there was no such thing in Ja-pan as the Yed-do sway or the post of Great Sho-gun. The Cho-shi-u clan was brought back to its right place with the Ku-ge, cleared of the charge that they had laid a plot to get hold of the Mi-ka-do; and the brave chiefs, as well as the young men who had run off to Eu-rope and our own land, were put in posts of trust.

The Yed-do clans were full of rage; they got their ex-Sho-gun to make war on Ki-o-to and get back what they had lost; but it was no use. A fight of three days took place, but the Sho-gun side lost and fled with their chief to O-za-ka, whose cas-tle was burned by the troops of Mi-ka-do's clans. He found a place on an A-mer-i-can ship and got at last to his home at Yed-do. Then, in spite of all that his clan-chiefs could do to urge him to keep up the fight, he held firm to this, that he would nev-er more make war on his lord, the Mi-ka-do. He gave up all thoughts of a pub-lic life from that day, and said the rest of his years should be spent as were those of the men of his caste. By this he saved Yed-do from the torch, which was lit for it when word was sent that the Sho-gun gave up all his claims; and by this he saved Ja-pan from a long home-war. A few clans still held out, but they were soon put down, and by the 1st of Ju-ly, 1869, the realm once more was a land of peace.

Then came that task that comes in the wake of all great home-wars when the side of a new cause wins: the Mi-ka-do and his new Court had to fit the old realm to the new state of things. All grades had their cries. One said send out the "brutes"; the Shin-to priests would have the Christians dealt with, the Bud-dhists put down, and the new rule set up by the pure Shin-to creeds.

It was the young men who, in spite of all the Sho-gun's threats, had learnt the speech, the thought and some of the ways of the Eu-ro-pe-ans, who took it on them-selves to set the Ku-ge right as to the "brutes," and to show the Mi-ka-do and Court, as well as the rest of the realm, how much it would be to the good of Ja-pan to make much of the folk from the West, and to take up with some of their thoughts and ways. They asked the am-bas-sa-dors or men who had been sent to Ja-pan to act for their na-tions, to go and see the Mi-ka-do. Two of them went, and the Ku-ge were won by the first sight of them and "made friends with the men they once thought were beasts." It was a hard task for the young men who set out to do this, for the folks were all much down on the strange men; and it was no small task to get them safe to Ki-o-to. A band of low-class youths fell on one train to slay them, but he who went first lost his head by the sweep of the sword of one of the brave young lords, who had made up his mind that come what might the Mi-ka-do and the Ku-ge should see what the Eu-ro-pe-ans were like.

A HAND CAR-RIAGE OR JIN-RIK-I-SHA.

Then a let-ter was sent out by one of these same brave young lords, that set forth to the Court, dai-mi-os and all the folks some of the new views on which it was their wish to base the new form of rule.

This is what the letter said: Since the Mid-dle A-ges our Em-per-or has dwelt with a screen in front of him and has not trod the earth. Naught of what went on in front of his screen got to his ear; his whole house was shut out from the world. Not more than a few lords of the Court could go near the throne. This is not like the laws of Heav-en; and now while we hold him none the less in awe and love, let us put off pomp and false forms and be plain and right in what we do. Ki-o-to is an out-of-the-way place and not fit to be the seat of rule. So let our lord move and make his home in O-za-ka, have his Court there and thus cure one of the hun-dred wrongs that have come to us from the past.

To speak of such a plan gave a great shock at first; but the Mi-ka-do did come out from be-hind his screen, and with the lords of the Court and dai-mi-os took an oath that things should be done by the voice of the folks; that the rough, rude forms of rule they had held to so long should be done with; and that the new ones should be fair and just to all. He said they would search the whole world for breadth and depth of thought, for sound, wise views; and for such arts and learning as would best aid them to build up the new Em-pire.

There has not been long to test this new plan yet; but there is no doubt that the Em-per-or and his staunch friends meant all they said and much more. Books and the news press were not shut down. The Jap-a-nese who wrote found they had naught to dread if they said what they thought. They were told to speak out that they might be a means to teach the folks what this new state of things was for and to help on in the good work. The Em-per-or would treat all men, e-ven those who had held to his old foes, on kind, just terms, and not a few of the To-ku-ga-wa clan were asked to take posts of note in the realm. To all the dai-mi-os of the lost cause he gave back rank and funds.

But day by day it came to be more plain to be seen that the realm could not rest in peace and reach the growth in the way of the new life it had learnt to hope for as long as feu-dal-ism should last. Clan strength would break that of the throne. This was what the press took up, and not a few of the dai-mi-os who had felt the same thing for a long while now saw that the time had come to act; and, led by the chief clans, they all sent word to the Mi-ka-do that they would give up their fiefs and their troops as the right of the throne, and be plain men from that time on. They said that in their new life one-tenth of the funds they had had would be all they should need, and the rest should be put in his own chests; for the realm was none too rich, and it cost much to put through all these new plans. This was set on foot by Prince A-kid-zu-ki, and ere long the whole 264 dai-mi-o gave up their fiefs and troops and vast wealth to be plain Ka-zo-ku (no-ble-men). Thus the lands, the great hosts of men-at-arms, and large tax went at once to the throne to help on the work of its new life to bind all parts of the realm in-to one whole, whose sole head was the Mi-ka-do. Yed-do, or To-ki-o, the East-ern cap-i-tal, came to be the seat of the Court plans for a rail-road were thought of; young men were sent to Eu-rope and this land to be taught Col-leg-es and schools in all the crafts and arts and lore known to the folks of the West were set up in the towns of Ja-pan, and folks who could teach were asked to go from Eu-rope and A-mer-i-ca to take charge of them. Scores of new ways were put in place of the old; and e-ven the Mi-ka-do came out and was seen by crowds of folks of all grades when the first trains were put on the Grand Trunk Rail-way from To-ki-o to Yo-ko-ha-ma.

GLOSSARY.

Spelled.	Pronounced.
Ad-zu-ma	Ad-zu-má.
Ai-no	Aï-nó.
A-kid-zu-ki	A-kid-zú-ki.
Am-e	A-mé.
Ash-i-ka-ga	Ash-í-ka-ga.
Au-ji-ro	Au-gí-ro.
Bi-wa	Be-va.
Bi-dat-su	Be-dát-sú.
Bu-ret-su	Bu-rêt-sú.
Chi-u-ai	Chi-ú-áï.
Chin	Shin.
Cho-shi-u	Chô-shi-ú.
Dai-mi-o	Dái-mi-ô.
Dis-hi-ma	Di-shi-ma.
Fu-ji-wa-ra	Fu-gï-wá-ra.
Fu-ku-i	Fu-ku-ï.
Gen	Gén.
Go-Dai-go-Ten-no	Go-Dái-go-Ten-nô.
Go-ro-za	Go-ró-sa.
Go-to-ba	Go-tô-ba.
Ha-ko-ne	He-kó-ne.
He-ro	Hê-rô.
Hi-de-yosh-i	Hi-dé-yos-si.
Hi-u-go	Hi-ó-go.
Hi-ye-zan	Hi-yé-zan.

Glossary

Spelled.	Pronounced.
Ho-jo	Hô-gô.
Hon-do	Hon-dú.
Ho-o	Hô-ô.
Ho-so-ka-wa	Ho-só-ka-wa.
I-bu-ki Ka-ma	E-bé-ki Ya-mâ.
Id-zu	Ed-zú.
I-ke-da	E-ké-da.
I-ki	E-ke.
I-se	E-sé.
I-ye-yas-u	E-yé-ya-shŭ.
Jim-mu Ten-no	Gem-mú Ten-nô.
Jiu-gu Ko-go	I-ïú-gu Kâ-gé.
Ka-i	Ká-i.
Kad-zu-sa	Kád-zu-sá.
Ka-ma-ku-ra	Ká-ma-kú-rá.
Ka-mi	Ká-me.
Ka-mo	Ká-mô.
Kash-i-wa-ba-ra	Kâsh-í-wa-ba-râ.
Ka-wa-dri	Ká-wa-dri.
Ke-i-ko	Ke-ï-kô.
Ki-na-i	Ke-ná-i.
Ki-o-mo-ri	Ke-ó-mo-ri.
Ki-o-to	Ke-ô-to.
Kir-ish-i-ma	Kir-ísh-í-ma.
Ki-u-shi-u	Ki-u-shí-u.
Ku-am-ba-ku	Kú-am-bá-ku.
Ku-an-to	Ku-an-tô.
Ku-ge	Ku-gé.
Ku-ma-so	Ku-má-so.
Ku-man-o	Ku-má-no.
Ku-sun-o-ki	Ku-su-nó-ki.
Mas-as-hi-ge	Ma-sa-shí-gé.
Mich-i-a-ri	Mi-shi-á-ri.

Glossary.

Spelled.	Pronounced.
Mi-ka-do	Mi-ká-dó.
Min-a-mo-to	Min-a-mó-to.
Mi-no	Mí-nô.
Mi-sa-za-ka Shi-ra-to-ri	Mi-sa-zá-ka Shi-ra-tó-ri.
Mi-to	Mi-tô.
Mo-ri-a	Mó-re-â.
Mo-ri-yo-shi	Mo-ri-yó-shi.
Mut-su	Moot-shoo.
Mut-su-hi-to	Moot-shoo-hi-to.
Nit-ta Yosh-i-sa-da	Nit-tá Yosh-i-sá-da.
Ni-pon	Ni-hon.
No-bo-no	No-bô-nó.
No-bun-a-ga	No-boo-na-ga.
O-jin	O-gin.
O-ki	O-ky.
Ot-su	Ot-su.
O-wa-ri	O-wá-ri.
O-za-ka	O-za-ka.
O-zu-mi	O-zu-mi.
Sa-ku-rai	Sha-ku-rái.
Sa-mau-rai	Sha-mu-rái.
Sat-su-ma	Sat-sú-ma.
Se-i-mu	Se-ĭ-moo.
Se-ki-ga-ha-ra	Se-ki-ga-há-ra.
Shi-ba-ta	Shi-bá-ta.
Shi-mo-sa	Shi-mô-sa.
Shi-na-no	Shi-ná-no.
Shin-to	Shin-tô.
Shi-ra-ki	Shi-rá-ki.
Sho-gun	Shô-gun.
Shik-ken	Shik-kén.
Su-jin	Shŭ-gin.
Sung	Shung.
Ta-chi-ba-na Hi-me	Ta-chi-bá-na Hy-mé.

Spelled.	Pronounced.
Tai-ko	Tai-kô.
Ta-i-ro	Ta-i-rô.
Tak-au-ji	Tak-á-ú-gi.
Ta-ta-ra	Ta-tá-ra.
Ten-shi	Ten-shí.
To-ki-ma-sa	Tó-ki-ma-sá.
To-ki-o	Tó-ki-ó.
To-ku-ga-wa	To-kú-ga-wa.
Toy-o-to-mi	Toy-o-tó-mi.
Tsush-i-ma	Tsu-shí-mâ.
U-ji	U-gi.
Us-u-i To-ge	U-súï Tô-gé.
Yosh-i-mit-su	Yosh-i-mít-sú.
Yosh-it-su-ne	Yosh-it-sú-né.
Yo-ri-i-ye	Yo-ri-í-ye.
Yo-ri-to-mo	Yo-ri-tó-mo.
Yu-ma-to-Da-ke	Yu-má-to-Da-ké.

ROUTLEDGE'S HISTORICAL COURSE.

IN WORDS OF ONE SYLLABLE. By Mrs. HELEN W. PIERSON.
Each book containing about 225 pages. With Illustrations and Maps
Price per volume, $1.00.

THE HISTORY OF THE UNITED STATES.

In noticing the "HISTORY OF THE UNITED STATES" the *New York School Journal* says :

"This book is well bound, printed on heavy paper, copiously illustrated, and most attractively written. There is no book in the market filling its place. It is purely a historical work (not a romance), comprising events from the commencement of the history of our country down to the present time. Mrs. Pierson has done her work well, and this is great praise, for it is a most difficult task to write history so as to be interesting to young people and yet keep out all but history. This work is here done, and for this we heartily commend the book."

HISTORY OF ENGLAND.

What Educators say of the Books:

"The one syllable 'History of the United States' has been used in my school with great success, and I regard it as a *most valuable book*, just filling a want I have long felt—an interesting account of our own country simple enough for beginners; the 'History of England' seems equally well adapted to young classes, and I shall take pleasure in using them in my own school, and in recommending them most heartily."—M. LOUISE COMSTOCK, 32 and 34 West 40th Street, New York.

HISTORY OF FRANCE.

The New England Journal of Education, says:

"The recent educational publications of George Routledge & Sons are worthy of special attention by educators. They include The History of England, The History of France, The History of Germany, The History of the United States, in Words of One Syllable, by Mrs. Pierson. These *four* books of history are written in a style that will make their use for general and supplementary reading not only interesting, but instructive to the young. The broad pages, printed in very large, open type, the beautiful and appropriate illustrations, make these books the best, on *historical subjects,* in the language."

HISTORY OF GERMANY.

The *New York Nation*, in noticing these histories, says:

"The *four* volumes by Mrs. Helen W. Pierson, repectively a History of the United States, of England, of France, of Germany, in words of one syllable, are clever performances, and calculated to interest the childish reader. . . . All these books are brought down to date.

HISTORY OF IRELAND

IN WORDS OF ONE SYLLABLE. By AGNES SADLIER. Fully Illustrated, lithographed cover, boards, $1.00.

Contains views of all the historically interesting towns and ruins, and portraits of the better known statesmen—from O'Connell to Parnell.

THE LIVES OF THE PRESIDENTS OF THE

UNITED STATES, IN WORDS OF ONE SYLLABLE. By Mrs. HELEN W. PIERSON. With Portraits and many Illustrations, $1.00.

Designed to acquaint young folks with the salient features in the lives of the Presidents, from Washington to Cleveland; and tells in a plain and succinct way of the course of the government since its formation. It is embellished with portraits of all the Presidents; and also gives portraits of the unsuccessful aspirants for the office; as well as of some of the ablest of the Secretaries.

HOME LESSONS; OR, LEARNING MADE PLEAS-

ANT BY MEANS OF PICTURES AND STORIES. Lithographed Cover, boards, $1.00.

Embraces nearly everything that a child desires to know from the alphabet to the wonders of science. It is, in fact, a veritable little folks' cyclopædia.

Specimen pages furnished on application.

GEORGE ROUTLEDGE & SONS,

9 Lafayette Place. New York.

www.ingramcontent.com/pod-product-compliance
Lightning Source LLC
Chambersburg PA
CBHW031818220426
43662CB00007B/699